TEACHING IN/BETWEEN
CURATING EDUCATIONAL SPACES WITH AUTOHISTORIA-TEORÍA AND CONOCIMIENTO

Leslie C. Sotomayor II
Texas Tech University

Curating and Interpreting Culture

VERNON PRESS

www.vernonpress.com

In the Americas:	*In the rest of the world:*
Vernon Press	Vernon Press
1000 N West Street, Suite 1200	C/Sancti Espiritu 17,
Wilmington, Delaware, 19801	Malaga, 29006
United States	Spain

Curating and Interpreting Culture

Library of Congress Control Number: 2021947189

ISBN: 978-1-64889-122-9

Cover designed by Antonio Howard.

Antonio M. Howard, Community Muralist

Bio

Antonio Howard (Peggy's son) is an autodidactic artist. At the young age of 15, he was incarcerated and sentenced to life in prison, where he served 26 ½ years. While in prison, he educated himself on the concepts and processes of visual art-making through instructional books. He writes, "Although I often dreamed of being an escape artist, as a visual artist, my paintings broke free of [prison] long before I did."

Released in 2018 and now living as a civilian here in Erie, he is committed to serving Erie and documenting his life through his paintings. Antonio is the 2019 recipient of Erie Arts and Culture's Emerging Artist Fellowship. He is a Teaching Artist through Erie Arts and Culture / Pa Arts Counsel, and since 2020 has participated in the creation of several murals throughout Erie including, the Whole Foods Co-Op mural; the Manus Sunoco Mural honoring 93-year-old veteran, educator, and Gannon alumni Luther Manus; The MHA Tree of Life mural; two City of Erie bandwagons; and a Purple Martin mural recently completed on behalf of Bayfront Eastside Taskforce. Antonio is also the author of three books: When A Child Is Worth More Than the Worst Mistake He Ever Made; A Black Man and A Spear(e); and Love Is When You Want The Best (For Someone Else). He sits on the board of directors for the Mental Health Association of Northwestern Pennsylvania, is a member of the steering committee for the Pardon Project of Erie County, and is an American Bar Endowment Pardon Fellow. He is also a core member of Erie's Participatory Defense, an Erie community organization that offers support to individuals and their loved ones navigating the criminal legal system. He is also past president of the CHROMA Guild, whose mission advances opportunities and access to resources for creative and cultural professionals of color in Northwestern Pennsylvania. The regional network builds both individual and organizational capacity by expanding equity and inclusion within the area's cultural and creative sector. In his day job, Antonio works as a paralegal with the Federal Public Defender.

Table of contents

List of figures

Abstract

This decolonial feminist teacher inquiry documents and analyzes my experiences teaching the undergraduate course *Latina Feminisms, Latinas in the US: Gender, Culture and Society.* The premise for this study was my initial research for my dissertation work. I interpret the seven recursive stages of Gloria Anzaldúa's conocimiento theory as transformative acts to guide my research design and teaching approach. I apply Anzaldúa's theories of autohistoria-teoría and conocimiento to curate educational spaces that decolonize White hegemonic academic canons and empower underrepresented learners who may experience a deep sense of not belonging in academia. I situate myself in the study as curator, and my practice of curator, as an agent of self-knowledge production and theorizing to create self-empowering learning environments. Teaching and learning from a feminist testimonio writing practice of theorizing experiences (i.e., autohistoria-teoría) is important to this work. I situate my testimonio in the introduction as an example of autohistoria-teoría. In my approach and experience from curating the *Latina Feminisms* curriculum, I witnessed transformational learning from the following: awakening, vulnerability, belonging, healing, and interconnectedness.

Dedicated to my children and grandchildren.
We are the past, the present and the future.

Acknowledgements

To my children: Christina Anne, Sterling Lance, Miles Avery, and Sophia Ana and my granddaughters: Carmen Alexandria and Camila Avayah, who are the greatest joys of my life.

I am deeply grateful to my ancestors, who paved the way for me today. May we remember we each have the power to create new stories for ourselves. With great love and affection, my hope and work are towards a greater, more loving, empowering and transformative today and tomorrow, for all people.

This book is but a marker in my journey, made possible by my hard work and the endless guidance, support and mentorship of phenomenal human beings in my life. These pages hold the imprint of those who have traversed my life in a myriad of ways and impacted my life profoundly. I thank my parents, Angel L.Sotomayor and Leidis (Leslie) Fayad Puente, for my life and for sharing the best of themselves with me. I am grateful to my mentor, Dr. Karen Keifer-Boyd, for the endless investment of her time into my work, who saw in me what I couldn't see in myself years ago. I am forever and continuously thankful to all of the humans in my life who have sat with me, listened, resisted, challenged, and been present with me on this journey of life; I am here because of you. I am grateful to Dr. Clemente Abrokwaa, Dr. Eric Ian Farmer, Dr. Christen García, Dr. Stevie Berberick, Jessica Namais, BJ Weaver, Dr. Ilayda Altuntas, Dr. Stephanie Cardona, Ana Fernandez, Bonnie Collura, Martha Jensen, Julie Porterfield, Dr. Anne Whitney, Dr. Eduardo Navas, Dr. Wanda B. Knight, and Dr. AnaLouise Keating.

Foreword
by
Dr. Christen Sperry García

No Representation is Representation:
Teaching Nepantla through Art Practice

1. Make art like a White man so that it can have value in the art world.

2. White artists are called "artists." Artists of color are called *Black artists, Latinx artists, Native American artists, Asian artists*, etc.

3. When asked to name five artists, many undergraduate art students will name five White male artists.

4. When asked to name five Latina/x artists, many undergraduates are unable to identify artists other than Frida Kahlo and Diego Rivera (there is, after all, a movie about them).

5. Art is not taken seriously if it has to do with cuteness, motherhood, feminist issues, or identity.

6. There are art history courses dedicated to *women* artists, but none to male artists because they are overrepresented in virtually every art history time period.

No Representation *is* Representation in Art Education

The above statements are among common themes pervasive in art school and the art world at-large. Artists of color are presently and historically unrepresented in the visual arts. As a result, there is a lack of scholarship written by and on art practitioners of color. This includes the art curriculum. In her *Studies in Art Education* article, Leslie Sotomayor argues:

> No representation *is* representation, meaning that when we (marginalized people) do not see parts of ourselves, our histories, and contributions reflected in the society, the institutions, and the canons of knowledge in which we live, our realization of not being represented generates a silent loudness or a gaping hole. (2019, p. 134)

The gaping hole that Sotomayor refers to is highly relevant in the field of art and education. Firstly, many higher education institutions do not require ethnic studies in their core curriculum. As a result, many students leave with an undergraduate degree centered on colonized knowledge. Students are offered limited perspectives on underrepresented groups, which is a disservice to White students and students of color, who do not see themselves in the curriculum. And if they do, the scholarship, in many cases, is written by White academics. This void or gaping hole is further exposed in examining arts education through a Critical Race Theory (CRT) lens. The *Palgrave Handbook of Race and Arts in Education* (Kraehe et al., 2018) applies CRT to arts education and examines the arts as property. More specifically, the authors argue that the arts are *White property*. White superiority appropriates art institutions, including schools, museums, and galleries. *What* (curriculum) is taught is a part of the art institution and, therefore, can also be argued as White property. However, while extremely relevant in the field of arts education in relation to race and representation, this handbook does not focus on Latina/x issues.

Moving from theory to practice, there are few curricular resources for arts educators on race and identity. For example, the *Art Education in Practice Series,* produced by the publisher Davis, is used to teach artists how to teach art. Addressing art education history, curriculum design, assessment, visual culture, and community art, they offer little representation of communities of color beyond issues of diversity and multiculturalism. This series offers little to no insight on borderlands or Latina/x perspectives, art histories, or curriculum development from Latino/a perspectives. In addition, some National Art Education Association's (NAEA) publications cover diversity and multiculturalism (Brown, 2011; Manifold et al., 2016), but do not discuss how systemic racism relates to art education. In teaching art education in higher education, one must look to other fields to address issues of race and identity: Women's Studies, Art History, and Latina/x and Chicana/x Studies.

While *Border pedagogy* (Giroux, 1991 & 2005; Kazanjian, 2011) and *borderlands pedagogies* (Leake, 2019) address race, representation, and use in-betweenness as a pedagogical site, they are not informed by Latina Feminism. Border pedagogy (Giroux, 2005) is not an arts-based teaching approach, but it uses the U.S./Mexico border to examine difference and struggle. More specifically, border pedagogy examines geographical, conceptual, and metaphorical borders to cultivate dialogue surrounding underrepresented groups, cultures, histories, and politics (Giroux, 1991; Kazanjian, 2011). In addition, border pedagogy is a call to action in which students conceptually cross borders to understand otherness and re-create their identities through border languages (Giroux, 1991). Lastly, border pedagogy examines underrepresented histories, narratives, and identities as a way to reframe hegemonic canons of knowledge (Giroux, 2005). Borderlands pedagogies, on the other hand, is a studio-based teaching practice wherein students and teachers come together to co-create knowledge through a visual methodology (Leake, 2019). Borderlands pedagogies examine issues of immigration, asylum-seeking, and border living through art and social practice. The results of this approach are visual artifacts, including drawings, photographs, text collages, image and text works. This art/teaching practice resists an *us versus them* mentality and highlights larger socio-structural systems that perpetuate oppression and racism. Borderlands pedagogies cultivate dialogue and promote listening, critical reflection, and vulnerability.

Sotomayor uses conceptual, geographical, and metaphorical borders, like border pedagogy, to promote dialogue on racial oppression, in-betweenness, and identity, similar to borderlands pedagogies. However, what Sotomayor adds is an autobiographical feminist teaching and art practice informed by the work of *frontizera* (border) queer Chicana, Gloria Anzaldúa (1987, 2009, 2012).

A Gloria Anzaldúa Informed Art/Teaching Approach

...Vivo en este estado liminal entre mundos, entre realidades, entre sistemas de conocimiento, entre sistemas de simbología. Este terreno fronterizo al umbral de la conciencia, o pasaje, esta entretela, es lo que yo llamo nepantla.

...I live in this liminal state between worlds, between realities, between systems of knowledge, between symbology systems. This liminal borderland terrain, or passageway, this interface, is what I call *nepantla*. (Anzaldúa as cited in Codex Nepantla, 2020).

For Anzaldúa, *nepantla* is an ideological space that exists living in-between two worlds. Sotomayor uses Anzaldúa's world of liminality that weaves between systems of reality, knowing, and symbolism. Though not a visual artist, Anzaldúa conceptualizes nepantla as a borderlands art practice. In *Luz en lo Oscuro: Light in the Darkness*, Anzaldúa & Keating (2015) outline a feminist conception of a *border artist* as a way to center art practice on living in-between worlds:

Border artists inhabit the transitional space of nepantla. The border is the locus of resistance, of rupture, and of putting together the fragments. By disrupting the neat separations between cultures, Chicana artists create a new culture mix, una mestizada. (p. 47)

The authors make productive the ambiguity, tension, and contradictions that occur living in-between worlds. Border artist and Chicana artist are synonymous as they are both marginalized groups of artists. Chicana artists mediate an active process of falling apart and coming back together through visual means. This process is a merging of two or more spaces into one.

Through autohistoria-teoría (see Appendix C), Sotomayor focuses on theorizing through creative acts that inhabit an uncomfortable in-between space of nepantla. While Anzadúa offers theories on border artist practices, Sotomayor puts them into practice through a *decolonial feminist curriculum and teaching approach*. She analyzes and applies *Anzaldúa's* writing on autohistoria-teoría, conocimiento, and nepantla (see Appendix C) to create both an art practice and pedagogical methodology. While there is a text that puts borderlands theories into teaching practice: *Teaching Gloria E. Anzaldúa: Pedagogy and Practice in our Classroom and Communities* (Cantú-Sánchez et al., 2020), it does not cover visual representation. If there were a series on Anzaldúa's teaching practices, Sotomayor's book would be an entire volume covering creative acts in education.

Importantly, Sotomayor's pedagogical approach centers on the experiences of both students of color and White students. Through uncomfortable conversations, journaling, and art-making, Sotomayor guides students through self-reflection. This process is relevant in institutions centered around students of color, such as Hispanic Serving Institutions (HSI) and Primarily White Institutions (PWI).

Fighting Racism in Arts Curriculum

Creating an anti-racist curriculum is about action. In order to do so, inserting writings and art by artists of color is simply not enough. Academia is a colonized space with many who are well-read in racism, decolonial theory, Critical Race Theory, etc. However, words alone do not radicalize people (Yani, 2020). Sotomayor states:

> Moving forward I believe that we each have a responsibility to engage with many of these social issues and conversations with action. Token representations and curriculum is not enough, it never was enough. Adding diverse individuals into curriculum is not enough. Engaging in uncomfortable conversations to impact transformation, healing, and awakening is necessary. (p. 83)

Entering into uncomfortable conversations provide a way to disrupt the White ownership of art and education and reframe art education using *othered* experiences and perspectives. It is through reading, making art, self-reflection, journaling, and more, that Sotomayor suggests is a way to transform oneself. Sotomayor resists the idea of Whitened art education by developing a decolonial feminist curriculum and teaching approach she outlines in this book. In doing so, her goal is to decolonize U.S. White supremacy through reading and art processes as an alternative to white canons of art education.

Sotomayor's curricular approach does not exclude non-artists, teachers, and students in higher education. Importantly, her *curadora* (see Appendix A) curriculum process is accessible to students regardless of background or discipline. This approach does not require specific art skills to engage, only an openness to self-reflection. Her work is interdisciplinary. It resides on the borders of art practice, Chicana/x and Latina/x studies, feminism, and education. In merging these boundaries, a way to reframe and represent arts education from a Latina nepantla perspective arises.

References

Anzaldúa, G. (1987). *Borderlands/la frontera: The new mestiza*, 1st ed. San Francisco, CA: Aunt Lute Books.

Anzaldúa, G. (2012). *Borderlands/la frontera: The new mestiza*, 4th ed. San Francisco, CA: Aunt Lute Books.

Anzaldúa, G., & Keating, A. (2009). *The Gloria Anzaldúa reader.* Durham: Duke University Press.

Anzaldúa, G., & Keating, A. (2015). *Luz en lo oscuro: Rewriting identity, spirituality, reality.* Durham, NC: Duke University Press.

Cantú-Sánchez, M., de León-Zepeda, C., & Cantú, N.E. (2020). *Teaching Gloria E. Anzaldúa: Pedagogy and practice in our classroom and communities.* Tucson, AZ: The University of Arizona Press.

Codex Nepantla (2020). Retrieved from http://www.codexnepantla

Gaztambide-Fernandez, R., Kraehe, A. M., & Carpenter, B. S. (2019). The arts as white property: An introduction to race, racism, and the arts in education. In R. Gaztambide-Fernandez, A. M. Kraehe, & B.S. Carpenter (Eds.), *The Palgrave Handbook of Race and the Arts in Education.* Cham, Switzerland: Palgrave Macmillan.

Giroux, H. A. (1991). Border pedagogy and the politics of postmodernism, *Social Text, 28,* 51-67.

Giroux, H. A. (2005). *Border crossing: Cultural workers and the politics of education.* New York, NY: Routledge.

Kazanjian, C. J. (2011). Border pedagogy revisited. *Intercultural Education, 22*(5), 371-380.

Leake, M (2019). The Social Practice of Borderland Pedagogies, *Art Education, 72*(4), 50-58. DOI: 10.1080/00043125.2019.1602499

Manifold, M.C., Willis, S. & Zimmerman, E. (2016). Culturally sensitive art education in a global world: A handbook for teachers. Washington D.C.: National Art Education Association.

Sotomayor, L.C. (2019). Uncrating Josefina Aguilar: Autohistoria and autohistoria-teoría in feminist curating of a muñecas series, *Studies in Art Education, 60*(2), 132-143. DOI: 10.1080/00393541.2019.1600221

yani [@zapatistarising]. (2020, June 6). can we also not pretend like reading alone will radicalize ppl, academia is full of well read racists & imperialists. [Tweet] Retrieved from https://www.twitter.com/zapatistarising

Young, B. (2011). *Art, Culture, and Ethnicity,* 2nd Edition. Washington D.C.: National Art Education Association.

Introduction

Autohistoria-teoría, a decolonial feminist writing practice of testimonio[1] conceptualized by Gloria Anzaldúa, is a way to create self-knowledge, belonging, and to bridge collaborative spaces through self-empowerment. Anzaldúa offers a proto-definition of autohistoria as a term to "describe the genre of writing about one's personal and collective history using fictive elements, a sort of fictionalized autobiography or memoir: and autohistoria-teoría is a personal essay that theorizes" (Anzaldúa & Keating, 2009, p. 578). Autohistoria-teoría is decolonial theorizing of one's own experiences, historical contexts, knowledge, and performances in creative acts (e.g., writing, artmaking, curating, educating, among other acts). What follows are examples of my decolonial feminist writing of my autohistoria-teoría testimonio to introduce why I teach in/between educational spaces.

You were born in this country.
You are an American citizen. Remember that.

I began college for the first time when I graduated high school a year early, at the age of 17. I remember walking onto the university campus for the first time feeling disconnected. It reminded me of when I was a young girl moving from a predominantly Hispanic neighborhood in New Jersey to a predominantly non-Hispanic neighborhood in Pennsylvania. Walking around the college campus, I again felt like I was on another planet and didn't quite belong. I only lasted there barely a year, failing out and deciding it would be better for me to marry my teenage sweetheart at 18. I remember my father taking me with him to the dean's office to discuss my situation. I have no recollection of what was said as I sat in his office, but I remember feeling invisible, not belonging anywhere.

I can hear the shattering of what I thought was reality, a deep desire
for something more had been building up in me.

After more than a decade from that day, a deteriorating marriage that I needed to leave, and three children later, at age 31, I walked onto a new

---

[1] Testimonio: a public testament of a lived or witnessed experience.

predominantly White campus, again, feeling like I didn't belong. During my first year as an adult learner pursuing my bachelor's degree, I needed to take an elective. One of the only classes that would fit my tight schedule hyphenated with motherhood was an Introduction to Women's Studies course. I had no idea what the class was or that there was even a field with this name.

I grew up in a traditional home, where my father worked outside of the home, and my mother stopped working outside of the home once she gave birth to me, her first child. I was shocked the first day of my Introduction to Women's Studies undergraduate course, as a Latina woman walked into my class and introduced herself as the professor for the course. This event radically changed my life. For the first time, I was witnessing what a Latina could be other than a mother, and I began to learn about my history as a Latina in the United States. From that day forward, I have aimed to curate my life through learning about my heritage, ancestry, U.S. context, and understanding why I have lived with a strong sense of not belonging. It was in the Introduction to Women's Studies class that I first heard the name of the Chicana feminist writer, Gloria Anzaldúa, among others. Many of the testimonies I read in *This Bridge Called My Back* (2002) resonated with me. Anzaldúa, through her writings, urged and inspired me to prioritize goals and practice the life I wanted as an artist; and to honor my story, which initiated a journey of self-empowerment and a sense of belonging to myself.

Spanish is my private language; I cross the threshold into English.

However, I quickly realized that this Introduction to Women's Studies class was unique. I sought to take every class from the small pool of Latina/o Studies classes available. In doing so, the stark reality became apparent, again—I felt I didn't belong in most of my other classes because the curriculum taught excluded experiences and voices of people of color from education, art, and curating. I became aware of what I did not possess; knowledge of myself, my history, art training, or a language and vocabulary to articulate myself through. English is, after all, my second language.

When I was five in public school kindergarten, one day, my mother was furious. I remember fragments as she angrily pulled me out of a meeting with teachers at the end of the school year. I remember her saying; "Mi hija nacío aquí, ella es Americana!!" (my daughter was born here; she is an American!!) and I never returned the following year. Instead, she registered me to begin in a private all-English speaking and teaching Catholic School. Later, I would understand what happened. My mother was offended that the public school I was attending was beginning to introduce the concept of Bilingual English as a second language class because of the changing local community from predominantly White to Hispanic. The elementary school implemented a trial program of pulling students out of the classroom for ESL classes. My teacher thought I would be a good candidate for this course since I was Hispanic, and Spanish is my first language. My parent's perspective was that at home, we spoke Spanish, and outside of home, my brother and I would pick up English in school, maintaining a bilingual practice. However, the school forcefully suggested the pulling-out-of-the-class for strategic ESL classes. My mother did not agree. She thought it was a horrible offense for the school to even suggest that I take a Bilingual English course. I remember having a difficult time understanding my English-speaking friends and teachers in Kindergarten. I had attended a Pre-Kindergarten school with predominantly Spanish-speaking teachers and students. My whole world was in Spanish until Kindergarten, where I still had some Spanish-speaking friends. My life consisted of family, friends, neighbors, church, and school as predominantly Spanish-speaking. Ironically, the elementary school, Horace Mann, in North Bergen, New Jersey, that I had attended briefly, changed their mission a few years after my mother pulled me out of the school. The elementary school developed a Two-Way Bilingual program where *all* curriculum is taught in both English and Spanish simultaneously. In 1997, the school received a grant for the program, radically changing the education and curriculum narrative to be facilitated in both the English and Spanish languages, and by 2002 becoming the exception of a pure dual-language magnet school.

When I arrived at my new private school, it was a major culture shock. I remember being scared and not knowing how to communicate with the other kids and the teachers who were English-speaking nuns. It was sink or swim. I had two Spanish-speaking friends in that elementary school; we clung together: Monica and Manuel. Eventually, I did learn English, but I always felt that I didn't belong. Everything about me and my life felt completely different. The way my mother did my hair, the shoes I wore, my lunches, and our extra-curricular activities. For example, I wasn't in cheerleading and did not know what that was.

> *I remember in fifth grade, my hair was turning curly,*
> *unlike everyone else's in my school.*
> *They pointed and laughed.*

Because the education I received in elementary through high school failed to include me, and when they tried to include me, it resulted in outrage from my mother; I grew up living in-be-tween and feeling like I didn't belong anywhere. People of color have been required to assimilate, look, speak, and act like their

White neighbors, educators, artists, and curators. However, in the preface of *This Bridge We Call Home,* Anzaldúa explains that the whole picture isn't just about displacing whiteness, although necessary, but also critically examining the layers of whiteness as not only critical of white identities, but of whiteness as an institutionalized way of thinking, educating, and moving in the world (Anzaldúa & Keating, 2002).

Next, college courses failed to theorize and include experiences like mine in the art field— again; I was feeling an all too familiar feeling that I have felt throughout my whole life, not belonging. It was the first academic setting I had with other Latino/a students, where we became vulnerable with each other through our *testimonios.* Just as important, I know the value of sitting in the classroom seats, witnessing a Latina enter the room and open a window into testimonios, poetry, listening and sharing lived experiences that rarely are voiced in academia. Based on my experiences of not belonging to myself, my autohistoria-teoría is a process for self-empowerment. I am compelled to share my experiences as a learner because I realize the value of knowing my histories and I believe other underrepresented learners like myself also may benefit from knowing their histories that have been silenced or marginalized in education.

Chapter 1

Curating feminist educational spaces: Definitions, lineages, and metaphors

As a Latina[1] student, I did not observe any representation[2] or acknowledgment of my ethnic background throughout my education from kindergarten through college.[3] I began to understand that my educational disadvantages, as an underserved student with Caribbean heritage attending overrepresented[4] educational institutions throughout my life, had helped me develop coping skills. One of the ways that I became self-empowered was to look to my ancestral roots from Puerto Rico and Cuba as places for self-discovery through testimonio art and writing. Because of this, I developed, implemented, and analyzed a decolonial feminist curriculum and teaching approach. Using this approach, I was able to theorize my own and my students' testimonios and

---

[1] I am an American-born, self-identifying Latina. My Caribbean heritage is a strong part of who I am and how I identify as well as my native Spanish tongue. Throughout my life I have struggled and grappled with the label of white-ness, being identified as either white or woman of color depending on where I am geographically positioned in the Caribbean and the U.S. and who is standing next to me. I may be 'white-passing' because of the hue of my skin, my Spanish bloodline, my 'good' English, my middle-class upbringing. But I may be a woman of color because of my olive tones, my phenotype features among other things that often are associated with the Latina stereotype, and my African and Taíno roots.

[2] No Representation *is* Representation is the name of an interactive art lecture I gave in class whereby examining activist art post 1960s social movements, as a class, we engaged in a dialogue about the things we know and do not know, critically reflecting on why.

[3] I use the term "Latina/o" rather than "Latinx" throughout my research work because the former term reflects Spanish linguistic conventions and is easily pronounceable by both bilingual and monolingual speakers. I find compelling the arguments made by Cristobal Salinas and Adele Lozano (2017) about the importance of avoiding imposing U.S./American social norms on other cultures by critiquing or ostensibly correcting the Spanish language with the use of a term like "Latinx." The term "Latinx" is non-existent in Spanish-speaking countries and is a U.S.-invented term serving a U.S. context (Salinas & Lozano, 2017; de Onís, 2017).

[4] Overrepresented: I use the term "overrepresented" throughout this study to refer to populations of people who have historically been portrayed within mainstream U.S. society and culture as privileged.

witness the students' processes of working with Anzaldúa's theories of autohistoria-teoría and conocimiento as I, and others, interpret her theories.[5]

I now realize that experiences like mine are not isolated nor uncommon; I witness it often in the classroom spaces I inhabit. When individuals are oppressed by systemic discrimination throughout their lives and through intergenerational transmission, they may come to believe the stereotypes, myths, and derogatory social narratives about their own group communicated through dominant media, education, institutions, and policies, among other means. Negative perceptions of oneself and one's cultural group normalize a sense of subordinate status and can lead to internalized oppression (Duran, 2013). Underrepresented students often experience a deep sense of disempowerment (Schmidt, 2005).

Feminist curating, however, has the potential to generate dialogue around a theme(s), feeling(s), or topic(s) that arises from lived experiences of discrimination and oppression (Reilly & Lippard, 2018).[6] My curricular curation decolonizes the White academic canons that have long governed course text selection in order to engage learners who experience a deep sense of not-belonging in academia.[7] My approach is based on the premise that decolonizing the U.S. academic canons of a White supremacist culture through the curation of readings and processes can challenge colonization. Through autohistoria-teoría and imagined futures, underrepresented, diversified voices can critically dismantle systemically internalized oppression to resist, challenge, and offer new possibilities for knowledge that have historically been silenced (Bhattacharya, 2013; Navas, Gallagher, & Burrough, 2017).

I critically reflected on and documented my own transformation as facilitator and researcher in developing and teaching the undergraduate course *Latinas in the United States: Gender, Culture, and Society*, otherwise known as *Latina Feminisms*. As both researcher and teacher, I developed and implemented a decolonial feminist educational approach that is in the genre of testimonio work. I approached the course curriculum by employing critical and creative forms of writing and art-based assignments. I curated the *Latina Feminisms*

---

[5] I do not italicize non-English words in order to maintain the decolonizing move performed by Gloria Anzaldúa: that is, to refuse to make that which is non-English appear as Other, as awry, as needing a different type of treatment (Johnson & Christensen, 2019).
[6] I situate "curator" in the same way as "teacher/educator." "Curate," in this research, is a verb meaning to pull together or sift through material such as teaching resources (Eeds & Peterson, 1991).
[7] I define Anglo or White Americans as those who are not of Hispanic or Latinx origin; who speak the English language, even if they are not necessarily of English or British decent; and who live in the United States (Barber, 2010).

syllabus around my autohistoria-teoría, testimonio, and Anzaldúa's (1999) book, *Borderlands The New Mestiza*. I chose to read and analyze *Borderlands* with students because it encompasses many things at once: poetry; history; myth; testimonio; languages, slang; intersections of race, class, sex, and gender; and spirituality. *Borderlands* aims to unpack and negotiate contradictions of fragmentation and wholeness while resisting modes of patriarchy. *Borderlands* is a border crossing of the self, community, culture, and society through multiple places, displacement, and dislocation. *Borderlands* is what Desirée Martín (2017) describes as "a productive state that signals agency and adaptability even as it honors the pain that comes with embodying contradiction" (para. 4). *Teaching In/Between* speaks to the traveling with and among educational spaces, what Patricia Hill Collins (2002) calls the insider/outsider. As an educator, I am consistently reminded of my intersectional identities that I am 'here and there', crossing back and forth between worlds.

The students' and my interpretations of the various sections of *Borderlands* took us on a journey through the seven transformative acts that comprise Anzaldúa's conocimiento theory. I refer to Anzaldúa's conocimiento theory as "transformative acts"[8] because, in my experience, her theory evokes deep reflections that intensify when engaged, changing *something* within us (see Appendix A for the glossary of terms). I describe the "acts" that comprise Anzaldúa's theory of conocimiento as "transformative" because each act is intended to bring about something and/or shed light on something. I also use the phrase "transformative acts" to avoid reproducing an ideology of hierarchy, as the use of steps or stages would suggest. Rather, I point to actions and performances that may be in collaboration with or independent of each other.

Transformative acts are crucial to avoid perpetuating a top-down hierarchy or reproducing a Eurocentric framework of knowledge and to restructure the relationship between the educator and learners as one of transparent and open communication. The facilitator adopts autohistoria-teoría and testimonio approaches intentionally. All underserved learners in higher education who have a sense of knowing and experience wounds/tensions/difficulty can benefit from this transformative curatorial approach. I use the phrase "transformative curatorial approach" to describe how I used Anzaldúa's conocimiento theory and the seven transformative acts to shape my curriculum (Anzaldúa, 2015). As a guide to decolonizing educational spaces through emergent cultures of curricula, Anzaldúa's theories of conocimiento and autohistoria-teoría examine the various contexts of learning through

---

[8] Acts: According to *Merriam-Webster* (2020), an "act" is "an action in order to bring something about, or in light of" (para. 1).

multiple paths of socio-politicized content value and diverse environments for education (Keifer-Boyd, 2019).

Learners who are underprivileged because of the entanglements[9] of socioeconomic status, race, ethnicity, sexuality, access to resources, education, and gender have little access to resources or representation in U.S. history and often experience discrimination (Knight, 2007). However, many learners do not know what they do not know. In the same way that I had no idea that other worlds and possibilities existed outside and within myself when I sat in an undergraduate classroom, learners most often enter the educational space without knowing what questions to ask, what histories to know, or even that their own lived experiences are valid sources of knowledge that no one else can know.

In this chapter, I define the terms I am using in my curatorial curriculum approach, the lineage I am working within and the metaphor that drives my approach. I believe that many learners share my sense of not belonging. This sense of not-belonging leaves learners disempowered and with painful wounds. In Chapter Two, I engage in a fictional conversation as I imagine between feminist writer Gloria Anzaldúa and art educator philosopher Maxine Greene and the connections I make between the two in reframing a curatorial curriculum approach that is liberatory and inclusive. In Chapter Two, I also define key ideas positionalities within transcultural spaces, healer/ing, curator/curadora. In Chapter Three, I unpack Borderland Theory in how I curated a *Latina Feminisms* curriculum for undergraduate educational spaces and share my decolonial feminist writing practice through the second part of my autohistoria-teoría. In Chapters Four and Five, I unpack my decolonial feminist teaching in seven transformative acts and my witnessing of transformative learning in the classroom space.

My approach creates awareness and offers an understanding of systemic internalized oppression in higher education. I define "systemic internalized oppression in higher education" as the microaggressions that underserved learners experience and internalize in their daily lives and that render them invisible in higher education. Systemic internalized oppression is a form of trauma that educators and learners often reproduce because it becomes a survival tactic (David, 2013). The journey of transformation is not about an end goal but rather about the process of learning to be patient with oneself and others. Fruit towards transformation begins to be born after learners are able

---

[9] "Entanglements" refer to the complex, overlapping relationships among race, class, and gender that affect the individual in all aspects of life. These concepts are difficult to pry apart because of their entangled state of existence (Knight, 2007).

to critically reflect and make decisions in their everyday lived experiences that support a sense of belonging, self-empowerment, vulnerability, healing, and empathy.

I define "curator" as an educator who is creating, implementing, and sharing a pedagogical approach that centers on co-creating knowledge with care and stewardship. As an educator curating a curriculum, I facilitated students' creation of temporary homes or places where they were able to enact processes for healing. As new narratives arose, these temporary homes became locations for education and decolonization, for crossing borders that were emotional, psychological, historical, and memory-driven.

A curator (a) intentionally uses curricular materials centered on underrepresented voices, or testimonios, that academic canons often elide; (b) prioritizes interconnectedness; (c) curates stories (autohistoria-teoría testimonio-theorizing); (d) creates a world; (e) plants a hypothesis for oneself and the world; (f) proposes a narrative or story; and (g) generates a new perspective. Through my testimonio, I interpreted Anzaldúa's *Borderlands* (1999) as a journey through the transformative acts of her conocimiento theory. Over the course of the transformative acts, the students and I navigated and curated our own autohistoria-teorías based on our beliefs and lived experiences using reflexive activities such as writing, art-making, discussion, research, collaboration, and testimonio. Feminist curricular curation is a reflexive process of education. I position education as a holistic process of facilitating knowledge-building with others through testimonios.

I believe that learners in my course and I, also a learner, came together with different knowledge, and we learned from each other. I met the learners in my course with the full intention that they, like me, had valuable knowledge, experiences, and insight that facilitated their own journeys and writing of autohistoria-teorías. I borrow from AnaLouise Keating's (2007) situating of new stories for transformative learning in which "we are interconnected" (p. 21). Too often, we as learners do not critically reflect on and think about the impact that we have on each other in our everyday lives. Noticing our interconnections requires us to confront notions of our independent selves and to recognize our commonalities.

Lineage of testimonios

The act of situating oneself within lived experiences and observations exists specifically within the Latina, Chicana, and Black women's movements (Keating, 2007). I sketch in this section parts of a lineage that connects lived experiences with social issues and movements. In discussing this lineage, I highlight the complexities of voices and various intersectionalities that arise from social issues such as race, socioeconomic status, gender, and sex. I present these pieces of lived experiences through a historical lens to illustrate the connections, and perhaps even overlap, in our similarities and differences. My hope is to show how underrepresented populations have forged opportunities for collaboration and solidarity through historical and contemporary social movements.

I define "autohistoria-teoría" as the testimonio act of theorizing lived experiences, my testimonio. Many Black women activists and writers have taken part in testimonio, including Sojourner Truth, who delivered her 1851 testimonio, "Ain't I A Woman?", at the Women's Convention in Ohio, and Ana Julia Cooper, Frances Beale, and Deborah King, who wrote and spoke about the concepts of "double jeopardy" and "multiple jeopardy" based on their lived experiences. Long before academics began using the vocabulary of theorizing and intersectionality,[10] Black women embodied intersectionality. Latinas have shared in the theorizing of lived experiences as well. For instance, Anzaldúa (1999), Cherríe Moraga (1997), Maria Lugones (2012), Norma Alarcón (1983), Linda Martin Alcoff (2005), Chela Sandoval (2013), and Mariana Ortega (2001) have all discussed Latina/o lived experiences in the United States in their much-needed studies on selfhood and identity. Only in the 1980s did Kimberlé Crenshaw (1989) coin the term "intersectionality" and Patricia Hill Collins (2008) make "black feminist thought" key to her influential conceptualization of standpoint theory. This is the lineage of lived experiences, testimonios, and the understanding of the complexities of multiple identities that women of color and other underrepresented populations in the United States recognize. Since the 1970s, as a result of liberation efforts in Latin America, testimonios have been understood as a form of writing that is part of a struggle of people of color for social issues and human rights such as education rights and knowledge production (Smith, 2010). I am positioning testimonio as an approach, a method, to conducting research and to bearing witness to learners' and my own experiences (Reyes & Rodríguez, 2012). Specifically, as an educator, I see testimonio as a pedagogical tool for learners to use in developing a critical frame that exposes structural marginalization. Learners are the readers, listeners, and narrators of testimonios.

I employ Maria Lugones's (2010) concept of decolonial feminism in conjunction with Anzaldúa's decolonizing framework to inform my work because of the libertine energy that Lugones's theory contributes. Decolonial feminism, according to Lugones (2010), is not only about pointing out or recognizing oppressions but also about preparing each other with the

---

[10] Intersectionality: Cultural patterns of oppression are not only interrelated but are bound together and influenced by the intersectional systems of society. Examples of this include race, gender, class, ability, and ethnicity (Crenshaw, 1989).

resources to avoid succumbing to our oppressions. Avoiding succumbing to our oppressions gives us hope for liberation, for the possibility to overcome oppression. Lugones's (2010) insight connects with Anzaldúa's[11] (1999) decolonizing framework because of Anzaldúa's resistance to and challenging of dichotomous hierarchy that she embodied in her work as Anzaldúa pressed back, muting dominant understanding. I apply Lugones's theory of decolonial feminism by discussing and approaching curricular curation as spaces for multiple understandings of realities. I envision community as affecting oneself and others simultaneously and acknowledge all life forms as valuable and humanized. As Chela Sandoval (2013) explains, when we dehumanize others, we move differently with and towards groups and individual peoples, precluding the possibility of liberation.

The practice of testimonio has heavily informed studies by U.S.-based scholars in areas such as critical race theory and Chican/o and Latino/a studies. Testimonio is a first-person oral and/or written account drawing on self-reflective, narrative practices intended to be made public, an urgent call for action regarding something to which one bears witness, to bring to light a wrong (Reyes & Rodríguez, 2012). Testimonio is different from other qualitative methods because it is both political and intentional, a unique expression of an approach used as a spoken account of oppression. Testimonio is an account told in the first person by a witness to particular events, a voice seeking empowerment through the voicing of their experiences. The narrator of a testimonio must thus include affirmations and empowerment intentions. Paulo Freire's (1970) *Pedagogy of the Oppressed* is an example of liberationist pedagogy that is not only liberating through the process of testimonio but is also politicized in the production of consciousness.

Testimonio also aims to name oppression and to interfere with actions against institutionalized marginalization. Las Madres de Plaza de Mayo, an activist organization in Argentina, formed in 1983 by mothers to protest the abduction of their children in the central plaza, is but one example of how a testimonio may serve as a call to action.[12]

---

[11] Gloria Anzaldúa does not describe or frame her work as decolonizing feminist work; however, I consider her work to fall within the genre and therefore am writing and analyzing the work from this perspective.

[12] The Madres de Plaza de Mayo is a community of mothers and human rights activists in Argentina that has remained active for almost three decades. Based on a qualitative analysis of archival and ethnographic data assembled through fieldwork, this article examines the crucial role emotions play in maintaining the Madres' embeddedness in territorially dispersed social networks. The Madres de Plaza de Mayo perform emotional labor within their movement to sustain their activism. The Madres' emotional

Lastly, although testimonios are individual accounts, they represent the voices of many affected by a particular social issue and may lead the narrator and listener to experience a cathartic epiphany that opens their eyes to a greater human consciousness (Smith, 2010). Since testimonio allows for the telling of a community story as well as an individual story, memory and the reconstruction of memories, play a significant role (Reyes & Rodríguez, 2012). Powell (2017) explains that as a location in art education and art-making, memory prods us to examine our own histories and view our individual and collective identity narratives as locations for knowledge and learning. Powell (2017) continues to explain that curated "[m]emories and their retelling are important to how we reflect on the past and push toward the future in art education" (p. 31). I believe this is where curating meets testimonio and autohistoria. Anzaldúa's definition of autohistoria-teoría incorporates fragments of "fictive elements" into the theorizing of the self as a way to make sense and meaning of our experiences. Testimonios do not need to be experienced entirely by their narrators. Rigoberta Menchú's testimonio is one example of how a writer can simultaneously be a narrator, informant, and cultural witness. Menchú wrote about her indigenous Guatemalan community's atrocities, and her testimonio was transcribed by anthropologist Elisabeth Burgos-Debray (Smith, 2010).

Ortega (2016) situates the multiplicitous self as a process of being in-between worlds that is fluid and intersectional. She writes, "embodied, [and] situates self in process that is being-worlds and being-between worlds and that is characterized by intersectionality and flexibility" (p. 77). Like Anzaldúa, Ortega points to lived experiences as complex and multiple but also simultaneous, as often we are both the participant and observer. Anzaldúa (2015) writes, "I simultaneously look at myself as subject and object" (p. 3). Anzaldúa further explains that wounding separates or disrupts the sense of self, una herida abierta (an open wound). However, Anzaldúa imagines the reality that although there is a painful wound, there is also the promise of a transformative healing process through the Coyolxauhqui Imperative, which she describes as a creative process and a vision of decolonization.

Ruth Behar, cultural anthropologist, storyteller, filmmaker, and writer, created a career based on her own nostalgia, the theorizing of lived experiences, and acts of connecting to others in these ways. In *Bridges to Cuba/Puentes a Cuba*, Behar (1995) compiles poetry, non-fiction, art, and

---

geographies emerge through their individual and collective practices in key places, which are themselves layered with emotions. Over the years, such practices have allowed the Madres to create widespread networks of activists and to sustain a social movement community that extends all across Argentina (Bosco, 2006).

testimonies to grapple with her multiple identities through diasporas, globalization, exile, and displacement. In the *Vulnerable Observer*, Behar (1996) exposes her vulnerabilities by writing candidly about her lived experiences as a woman at the intersection of U.S., Cuban, and Jewish cultures. In *Traveling Heavy* (Behar, 2013), she dives into her privileged position as both immigrant and traveler, as well as the tensions between displacement and home. Behar's work constitutes a prolific canon of anthropological writings, personal writings, poetry, novels, teaching reflections, and visual arts. Her work, in my opinion, is decolonizing in nature, as it seeks to break down the psychological, theoretical, and perceived borders that she grapples with in her personal life. She shares her vulnerabilities with others in the world as a way to awaken consciousness, to empower.

Embodying feminist decolonial education

I situate my curatorial approach to decolonizing academic canons as a site for generating emergent curriculum structures that are "forward looking, with an open and flexible organization of undefined content for unknown future contexts" (Keifer-Boyd, 2019, p. 75). I apply Keifer-Boyd's (2019) concept of cultures of curriculum to Anzaldúa's seven transformative acts because both are a process of evolved critical reflection: a process of questioning content (whom, where, when) and seeing the privileging of particular voices and structures for learning, teaching, and curating as changing and permeable. In other words, the curriculum is not fixed but fluid, organic, and ever-evolving to meet the needs of a particular moment in time. I have come to observe something very significant: My personal practice, theorizing, spirituality, facilitating, living—is an act of decolonizing in itself. It does not need a label because the work, the manifestations of my lived experiences and theorizing of how I move, work, speak, teach, and engage in the world, is proof of a decolonizing process in motion from the margins.

I see decolonization as a process that requires time and is filled with complex questioning. Who or what determines when decolonization occurs? How is decolonization occurring? Decolonizing— to decolonize—is a process that moves beyond a curriculum and classroom experience to affect invisible areas of human experience. Decolonization affects our perspectives of ourselves and others, the everyday walk of life, interactions, and critical self-reflection and questioning of the world as we inhabit it daily. The term "decolonizing" is limiting but important. Furthermore, the concept is problematic because it is situated in the reparations of Indigenous lands in the United States (Tuck & Yang, 2012). Therefore, the power structures that U.S. politics and society have been built on are settler colonialism cemented in settler-native-slave narratives, enact further forms of oppressions rather than eliminate them (Tuck & Yang, 2012).

However, my attempt here is to initiate an approach for decolonizing, which hopes to interrupt the current canon by situating the individual as empowered and affecting collective change. I am aware of the problems that this also brings with it, the baggage of decolonization efforts through social justice perspectives for curriculum as a "metaphor for things we want to do to improve our societies and schools" (Tuck & Yang, 2012). This valid point of "metaphorizations of decolonization makes possible a set of evasions...." is problematic at best because of the complexities it represents in forwarding and propagating further settler colonialism (Tuck & Yang, 2012, p. 1). Furthermore, I posit that we need to confront these complicated entanglements in our classrooms; in my experience so far, predominantly white institutions (PWI) failings of unpacking these contradictions are detrimental to our individual and collective consciousness for one. Secondly, underrepresented populations who are already on the fringes are in need of validation and tools to understand and actively engage in their own autohistorias.

The Banyan tree: Toward a sense of belonging and self-empowerment

Karen Ikas and Gloria Anzaldúa explored feelings of not belonging in an interview Ikas conducted that appeared in the second edition of Anzaldúa's (1999) *Borderlands*. Ikas asked Anzaldúa, "How do you see this intercultural[13] situation with regard to the Chicano culture and the Anglo-Americas influence?" (p. 234). Anzaldúa replied:

> In that context, one particular image comes into my mind: the Banyan tree. It is a tree that is originally from India but which I saw in Hawaii first. It looks like a solid wall. When the seeds from the tree fall, they don't take root in the ground. They take root in the branches. So, the seeds fall in the branches, and it is there, above the earth, where the tree blooms and forms its fruits. And I thought, that is where we are getting it. Instead of going to the roots of our Hispanic or Chicano culture we are getting it from the branches, from white dominant culture. I mean, it is not that I reject everything that has to do with white culture. I like the English language, for example, and there is a lot of Anglo ideology that I like as well. But not all of it fits with our experiences and cultural roots. And that is why it is dangerous not to know about your own cultural heritage at all, because then you don't have the chance to choose and select. (p. 234)

---

[13] Intercultural: The occurrence between or involving two or more cultures (*Merriam-Webster*, 2019).

Anglo-patriarchal narrative that many underrepresented students at U.S. universities experience. Strains of the Banyan tree that Anzaldúa observed in Hawaii also grow in parts of Latin America and the Caribbean, called Ceiba in Taíno. They grow, too, throughout the places my family lives in Cuba and Puerto Rico. Scholars credit inventor Thomas Edison with the planting of the first Banyan tree in the United States (Cosden & Newman, 2015). In the United States, this first Banyan tree is seen as something uprooted and exotic, disconnected from its land, allegedly brought in and planted by a famous White male. The arc of this narrative is too familiar to underrepresented college students of color. It echoes and reflects the disconnection that I experience on campus as a student and an instructor. Racism and internalized racist "perceptions [are] an interpretive process conditioned by education" (Anzaldúa & Keating, 2009, p. 131).

I use the Banyan tree as a metaphor to convey White narratives of privilege and racism that exoticize and oppress others. The Banyan tree is an epiphyte, as its seeds germinate in the crevices of a host(ile) tree. As the Banyan tree grows, it produces aerial roots that hang down and take root wherever they touch the ground. When the Banyan tree is at home, the host and seeds thrive, and when the tree is colonized, the seeds struggle to survive. In the same way, in order for learners to connect to their entangled historical and cultural roots and to thrive, educators need to curate environments of decolonization (Anzaldúa & Keating, 2009).

The Banyan tree metaphor

Anzaldúa's theories of autohistoria-teoría and conocimiento, when applied to the curation of art educational spaces, can address learners' deep sense of not-belonging and the wounds that learners have experienced. I believe that by using Anzaldúa's theories, students are able to process and recognize the legitimate reasons for their feelings. Many learners who have a deep sense of not-belonging experience their displacement as Anzaldúa describes it: "home— ethnic roots may not be as clear-cut as those connected to the land, nor as portable and potable as the diasporas roots clinging to immigrants' feet and carried from one community, culture or country to another" (Anzaldúa, 2015, p. 67). Like the ornamental fruits on white Banyan tree trunks, underrepresented people lead lives disconnected from their roots. Anzaldúa's arboreal illustration of how Anglo-American culture has influenced Chicano culture, or underrepresented populations, is a poignant metaphor for the concerns that this study addresses.

Systemic institutions and Eurocentric White populations have historically marginalized, oppressed, enslaved, and deemed inferior underrepresented people in the United States, making it difficult for underrepresented people to blossom in society and culture. Similarly, for generations, it was believed that the Banyan tree did not flower. However, scientific research by Timothy Laman (1995) showed that the Banyan tree bears fruit that is wrapped in thick layers of fruit flesh. When the fruit flesh is cut open, the many pink blossoms growing inside the flesh become visible. The Banyan's flowers do blossom but only inwardly, such that the flowers cannot be seen from the outside. I draw a parallel between the inward-blooming flowers and conocimiento's transformative acts. Both constitute inward transformations enacted as a form of spiritual manifestation through active participation in life (Anzaldúa, 2015). The Banyan tree, the root system, fruit, and flowers are all interconnected, a living, visual metaphor for spiritual practice as awareness that all things are interconnected. In fact, the pollination that occurs with the Banyan tree occurs inwardly, as Banyan wasps pollinate the fruit (Laman, 1995). I draw a connection between these Banyan wasps and the curation of new perspectives and academic canons as pollinating and germinating seeds towards transformations *from the inside*. Because the transformation, the work, is being done on the inside, to the naked eye, it may not be visible until it needs to be. I correlate this with my feminist curatorial approach, wherein observations of learners are limited during a semester because transformation is a process, not an end fruit. The process is cyclical and ongoing. The strength of the Banyan tree means that the tree has the ability to survive and grow for centuries, tolerating drought. When the Banyan seeds germinate, the roots grow down towards the ground, strangling the host tree. The trees grow laterally, with every trunk connecting either directly or indirectly to the primary trunk (Laman, 1995).

My aim is for underrepresented students to perceive themselves in academia and that this work will help educators curate effective teaching/learning environments that represent a variety of learners. The position of underrepresented students in academia in relation to their host campuses—as influenced by social capital, socio-economic status, marginalization, and stereotyping—is documented in the quantitative research conducted by Hurtado and Carter (1997) and Strayhorn (2012). Strayhorn (2012) investigated the impact of underrepresented students' intersectional realities on their sense of belonging (or lack thereof) at predominantly Anglo campuses (the Banyan tree).

It is important for us educators and learners, who continually feel a sense of in-betweenness and not-belonging, to learn methods to validate our experiences and reconstruct our identities with agency. It is equally important for art education and academia as a whole to have a process for understanding and supporting the learning experiences of students from underrepresented populations. The inclusion and facilitation of learning experiences that resist and challenge Anglo culture empower underrepresented students to reconnect with their cultures and cultivate their own roots that run deep in the earth. As part of the development of a curriculum, I explored how curating a syllabus using Anzaldúa's theories of autohistoria-teoría and conocimiento decolonize knowledge, foster self-empowerment, and facilitate transformation.

Chapter 2

Facilitating conversations between Gloria Anzaldúa and Maxine Greene: Theorizing within creative acts and art education

In this chapter, I construct an imagined conversation between art educator Maxine Greene and feminist writer Gloria Anzaldúa, discussing pedagogy in conjunction with creative acts and transformation to visualize a new perspective for educational environments. I also contextualize transcultural spaces, healing, and curadora/curator in my curatorial approach for curriculum in this chapter to better delineate my positionality within these frameworks.

Curating undergraduate environments with Anzaldúa's theories of conocimiento and autohistoria-teoría uses creative acts towards transformation and awakening consciousness through the healing of our wounds. Curating spaces where vulnerability and exposure of the wounds are shared, learners bear witness to each other's internalized pain. Anzaldúa explains that artists "bear witness to what haunts us, to step back and attempt to see the pattern in these events (personal and societal), and how we can repair el daño (the damage) by using the imagination and its vision" (Anzaldúa, 2015, p. 10). Through the creative acts, pain, trauma, and shadows are exposed, and a necessary fragmentation is enacted. The transformative acts of conocimiento and autohistoria-teoría encourage healing and integration of the self. The concept of transformative learning toward interconnectedness has also been important to the philosophy of aesthetic education (Greene, 1978, 1995).

Aesthetic education philosopher Maxine Greene (1995) explores concepts of possibilities, imagination, and interconnectedness towards transformation through art education. Her concept of an emancipated pedagogy which merges art and aesthetics as one education that empowers students and "allows them to read and to name, to write and to rewrite their own lived worlds" seeks to create inclusion and the making of "some common world" (Greene, 1995, pp. 147, 135). The similarities I connect between Greene and Anzaldúa are notions of creativity and imagination[1] weaving ideas and art for decolonizing canons and towards transformation. Greene (1978) defines art and aesthetic education as worlds that facilitate reflection and awareness in order to create meaning and new possibilities. She explains the possibilities for educators to "move more and more persons into the imaginative mode of awareness, as we free them to make their own visions real" (Greene, 1978, p. 196). Greene (1995) addresses a larger picture of art education advocating for active teaching in order to inspire active learners. She explains that imagination is an integral part of teachers' lives and learners' experiences to see new paths for learning, consciousness work, and empathy (Greene, 1995).

I define creative acts as manifestations of deep expressions, meaningfully interwoven experiences between the body, mind, soul, and spirit. Through the acts of writing, reading, storytelling, and other creative acts, the Self[2] is in the making. The making of the Self through creative acts is layered as it facilitates the making sense of ourselves, "our lives and our place in the world" and allows for healing (Anzaldúa, 2015, p. 177). I interpret both, Anzaldúa (1999) and Greene (1995) to employ art (creative acts) and imagination as tools towards transformative social change through liminal spaces.[3] Creative acts as a concept and action in creating offer the possibility to re-imagine and re-construct the stories and images, the symbols and narratives that shape a person's consciousness, not as an endpoint but towards new experiences. Curating is both a concept and an action of suturing together narratives, symbols, and images in the imagination and breathing them into being in the world. The creative acts are a quest for meaning from the whole being. The arts or creative acts are part of the healing process, as Anzaldúa explains: "I believe in the transformative power and medicine of art" (Anzaldúa, 2015, p. xxxii).

I juxtapose Anzaldúa's theories of conocimiento and autohistoria-teoría with Maxine Greene's (1978, 1995) emancipatory pedagogy in art education. Greene, similar to Anzaldúa, reaches beyond theorizing and creating environments for

---

[1] I see similarities between Greene and Anzaldúa's theories but Anzaldúa dives deeper into issues of entangled realities, healing, and spirituality as Women of Color and modes of consciousness. For example, "Speaking in Tongues: A Letter to Third World Women Writers," "Creativity and Switching Modes of Consciousness," "Haciendo caras, una entrada," "Bearing Witness: Their Eyes Anticipate the Healing," and *Light in the Dark/Luz en lo Oscuro: Rewriting Identity, Spirituality, Reality* (Anzaldúa, 2015).

[2] I capitalize Self as Anzaldúa does in describing the making of Self (Anzaldúa, 2015).

[3] Liminal spaces are defined as a crossing through a threshold, from what has been to what will or could be; leaving something behind and the process of becoming something else (Anzaldúa, 2015).

awareness but expands the crossings into active and critical self-reflective work to rewrite one's own empowered stories and engage in a healing process. Her emancipatory pedagogy towards freedom specifically addresses the inclusion of groups of people and ranges of media and arts which have historically been excluded from the art education canon (Greene, 1995). Furthermore, she posits that engaging with "pluralities of persons" may inspire individuals to find their own images, visions within an array of arts,[4] experiencing "all sorts of sensuous openings" (Greene, 1995, p. 137). Greene writes,

> Yes, it should be education for a more informed and imaginative awareness, but it should also be education in the kinds of critical transactions that empower students to resist both elitism and objectivism, that allow them to read and to name, to write and to rewrite their own lived worlds. (Greene, 1995, p. 147)

Anzaldúa, through her theory of autohistoria-teoría facilitates a coming together of fragmented lived experiences with a holistic perspective including the arts; which resists the traditional notion of art inhabiting a hierarchal privileged world. Anzaldúa's theories of autohistoria and conocimiento are an embodiment and theorizing in practice through everyday lived experiences. The transformative acts of the conocimiento process initiates conscious work—where the artist (educator, learner, curator, writer, performer, musician) embodies the creative acts (likened to a shapeshifter or shaman) and then manifests the creative work.

Through her creative act of writing *Borderlands,* Anzaldúa (1999) imagines (shapeshifts), embodies, and puts forth a healing process in cultivating a new mestiza consciousness. I interpret Anzaldúa's concept of the new mestiza[5] consciousness, manifested in *Borderlands* (1999), as an example of the process of healing through the creative acts while embodying her autohistoria-teoría. In doing so, Anzaldúa is the teller, knower, and listener simultaneously and makes the Self. I connect my interpretation of Anzaldúa's (1999) concept of the new mestiza consciousness to Greene's (1995) pedagogy that empowers learners to reflect critically, be present, and appreciate both learner and educator as curious seekers and for questioning.

---

[4] Maxine Greene (1995) includes in her definition of a range of media such as written and spoken language, riddles, poems, stories, fictions, dreams, novels, paint, pastels, clay, stone, melodies, dissonances, pulses of sounds, music, body in motion, dance, making shapes, exerting effort, articulating visions, and moving in space and time.
[5] Mestiza: acknowledging the mixture of bloodlines one is made up of.

Creative acts offer the possibility to re-imagine and re-construct the stories and images, the symbols and narratives that shape a person's consciousness. A holistic experience is a connection between the body's soul, mind and spirit. Artist Liliana Wilson (2011) describes her artworks as images surfacing as she has imagined and experienced them, representing issues of ancestry, gender, immigration, disappearances, socioeconomic, hopelessness. Her work is one of naming the invisible, calling out for social justice, as a form of testimonio. Wilson explains her artwork as narratives of atrocities that she has witnessed throughout her life, an illustration of the interconnectedness of oppressions. For example, her pencil on paper artwork, *Denial* (1997, see Figure 2.1), illustrates a woman covering her eyes in order not to see the atrocities being committed in front of her. She writes,

> I feel that there is so much denial because of the socioeconomic systems that are in place in the world today: the way women disappear, or are abused by their spouses; the poverty; the contamination of the planet; and so many more atrocities committed against us because of gender and poverty. (Wilson, 2011, p. 11)

The arts or creative acts are part of the healing process, as Anzaldúa explains: "I believe in the transformative power and medicine of art" (Anzaldúa, 2015, p. xxxii). Creative acts instigate a process towards healing.

Figure 2.1. *Denial* (1997), pencil on paper by artist Liliana Wilson. Used with permission.

Gloria Anzaldúa's theory of conocimiento and autohistoria-teoría

Conocimiento, the Spanish term for knowledge or consciousness, is a theory developed by Anzaldúa through the process of grappling with her own identity, history, heritage, and feelings of not belonging (Anzaldúa, 2015). Conocimiento, according to Anzaldúa, can be described as a type of spiritual inquiry toward self-love and validation (Anzaldúa, 2015). Anzaldúa was "driven by the desire to understand, know, y saber [and know] how human and other beings know. Beneath your desire for knowledge writhes the hunger to understand and love yourself" (Anzaldúa, 2015, p. 121). Conocimiento's transformative acts can be interpreted to symbolize the seven chakras or energies which, according to Eastern philosophy, hold our mind, body, and soul in balance (Anzaldúa, 2015). Anzaldúa explains that the seven transformative acts are within each other and the struggle between the knower and the shadow places that exist in us; places that are dark, repressed, and full of pain. The transformative acts are processes of dying and being re-born within oneself repeatedly and in various places in our lives.

Autohistoria, the creating of one's own story with agency, occurs in the fifth of the seven transformative acts of conocimiento, creating a new story. Anzaldúa further expands the fifth transformative act into her theory of autohistoria-teoría, the theorizing of one's fragmented lived experiences as a reframing. The deep critical self-reflectiveness of autohistoria redeems individuals who have often felt a sense of not belonging, been excluded, and silenced. The power to curate new ways of thinking from lived experiences and connections to others provokes social transformation. Throughout the seven transformative acts of conocimiento and autohistoria-teoría, curation is necessary to gather the valued aspects of one's life in order to be complete and to omit or sever that which does not serve the individual.

Seven acts of conocimiento

The transformative acts of conocimiento awaken consciousness and, in doing so, teach empathy and self-love. Anzaldúa writes that the premise of the conocimiento theory is the root word, conocer, to know, and it is the connections through knowledge that facilitate transformation or what she calls "its connection with activism" (Anzaldúa, 2015, p. 234). Anzaldúa's conocimiento theory underlies what I call seven recursive transformative acts: (a) arrebato susto, (b) nepantla, (c) Coatlicue, (d) reframing, (e) autohistoria-teoria, (d) renewal, and (f) nepantlera.

In each of the transformative acts, I forge careful curating necessary in order to grow new dialogue that decolonizes the host campus. Although the transformative acts are not linear, they have a core catalyst beginning with the stages of fear and the rupture leading to nepantla, a realm of in-between-ness, where the things that once felt or were thought to be stable, all of a sudden are not. Various stages can occur concurrently, and what is learned or made aware is called conocimientos (Anzaldúa, 2015). Anzaldúa explains, "By redeeming your most painful experiences, you transform them into something valuable, also para 'compartir' or share with others so they, too, may be empowered" (Anzaldúa, 2015, p. 117). The significance of conocimiento is to transform realities and heal through our wounds. Anzaldúa developed her conocimiento theory for years through her lived experiences and witnessing of others' lived experiences. I draw upon Anzaldúa's conocimiento theory to develop my research and curriculum design with each recursive transformative act.

Arrebato susto

The transformative path of conocimiento theory did not emerge until after Anzaldúa published *Borderlands/La Frontera* (1999), embodying what she described as forms of spiritual activism via creative acts (Anzaldúa, 2002). Her Borderlands theory is an over-arching theory or epistemology housing many of her other theories that she subsequently developed until her unexpected death in 2004. As I reread *Borderlands/La Frontera* (1999), I interpret Anzaldúa's concept of autohistoria theory through *Borderlands* as a map of the transformative acts in her conocimiento theory, where each transformative act is a marker of consciousness awakening life cycle throughout her book. For example, she begins *Borderlands* at the Mexico/U.S. border, where she feels pain, and wounded, which I interpret as the susto/arrebato (uneasy, restless, fear), the first transformative act of Anzaldúa's conocimiento process. As the reader, I found the first page jarring, forcing me to confront the past and present. Anzaldúa situates the border between Mexico and the United States as an open wound between the global south and north. She writes:

> The U.S.-Mexican border, es uno herida abierta where the Third World grates against the first and bleeds. And before a scab forms it hemorrhages again, the lifeblood of two worlds merging to form a third country-a border culture. (Anzaldúa, 1999, p. 25)

Mirella Vallone (2014) examines Anzaldúa's concepts of wounds, healing, and transformation by considering her works, *This Bridge Called My Back* (1981), *Borderlands/La Frontera* (1987), and *This Bridge We Call Home* (2002) as markers or steps through the conocimiento stages (Vallone, 2014). Vallone (2014) maps the conocimiento process through three of Anzaldúa's books as an epistemological framework of the seven transformative acts for spiritual inquiry, activism, and healing through an embodiment of the creative acts. Vallone (2014) analyzes Anzaldúa's work centered on the mestiza's body as a necessary catalyst for inner transformation and new consciousness (Anzaldúa, 2015; Vallone, 2014). I critically engage with *Borderlands* (1999) as a framework to decenter white patriarchal academic canons and curate a feminist approach towards community building by developing and activating new ways of thinking with learners. Through the embodiment of creative acts, autohistoria-teoría, and conocimiento towards healing, belonging, and transformation, social change is imagined. I have critically engaged with *Borderlands/La Frontera* (1999) as the foundation for my research in the *Latina Feminisms* course to extend beyond mestiza bodies to include individuals who have felt a sense of not belonging and systemic internalized oppression in higher education.

The conocimiento process is instigated from a spiritual hunger growing deep within ourselves, a yearning to be our authentic selves while experiencing a sense of not belonging (Anzaldúa, 2015). Often nature or life's course will guide us to question and desire to understand our realities and not continue living day to day in desconocimientos or deconocer (willed ignorance or not knowing). Our path in conocimiento insists that we confront our shadows (the things that reside deep within ourselves) and our desconocimientos, the things we do not know, whether in ignorance or deliberate, that have distorted our realities. Like the Banyan tree, bondage that restrains us from being who we really are results from the cultural and societal constraints we have faced, the dominant world views. These constraints affect our balance with the body, mind, and spirit. The shaking of self that occurs is a core identity crisis. It arises from a deep desire to know more about ourselves, evoking a spiritual quest.

Part of Anzaldúa's vision for peace and love of self and others comes via the pursuit of balance through spiritual practice. For Anzaldúa, spirituality is a perspective, what she calls a symbology system, and "[t]hrough spirituality we seek balance and harmony with our environment" (Anzaldúa, 2015, p. 39). I notice my shifting and merging with Anzaldúa's theories as I write my own views into her writing. Anzaldúa's unique inclusion of spirituality within the theory is a crucial component with layers including la naguala, or shapeshifting as a form of imagining and embodying the words that are then written, and continuously relational "serving as the conduit through which awareness is continuously achieved, embodied" (Zaytoun, 2015, p. 82). Because of a desire to understand oneself, circumstances in our life will arise that unveil aspects of who we are and our understanding of our realities, these inside and outside, private and public realities and contradictions seek balance within ourselves. Anzaldúa writes: "Although contemporary theories of identity leave out our innermost spiritual core identity, I'm interested in the connective membrane between the interiority and the exteriority of subjectivity" (Anzaldúa, 2015, p. 36). Often painful lived experiences are a catalyst for transformation, which

Cherrie Moraga defines as a "theory of the flesh," born out of necessity (Moraga & Anzaldúa, 2002, p. 23). Because of the force that occurs in shaking our core perceived realities, the experiences catapult an individual into nepantla, a crossing.

Nepantla

Nepantla is a Nahuatl word from the native southern Mexican people meaning the "space between two bodies of water, the space between two worlds" (Anzaldúa, 2015, p. 237). Nepantla is a tumultuous place, a remolino (whirlwinds), that is in transition as one transforms the self. Often, underrepresented learners feel the in-between-ness as "home, family, and ethnic culture tug you back to the tribe, to the chicane indigent you were before, the anglo world sucks you toward an assimilated, homogenized, whitewashed identity" (Anzaldúa, 2015, p. 126). Nepantla begins with an ending—a rupturing in one's life that can occur at any given moment, for any reason. Perhaps a traumatic life experience shakes everything you understood about your reality, suddenly calling your understanding into question. It is where one questions your cultures, identities; the very foundation of your life (Anzaldúa, 2015). Nepantla, the second transformative act in a conocimiento process, occurs after a shock, a susto, (fear) shakes you to your core and your faculty is awakened (Anzaldúa, 2015). It is only then that "éste arrebato, the earthquake, jerks you from the familiar and safe terrain and catapults you into nepantla, the second transformative act" (Anzaldúa, 2015, p. 122).

Nepantla is a crossing over from what has been to what will be—a threshold where realities are made visible as multiplicitous and dimensional (Anzaldúa, 2015). In other words, reality is relative, and within realities, we have choices to perceive realities in different ways. Like Shamanism, parts of ourselves are awakened, accessing "spiritual realities unseen by those whose awareness focuses entirely on the ordinary reality of daily life" (Anzaldúa, 2015, p. 32). Realities are exposed through curated learning spaces for underrepresented people when violence, trauma, and "other colonial abuses affect our self-conceptions," rupturing our psyches and identity (Anzaldúa, 2015, p. 87). It is through nepantla that one may enter or "tap 'el cenote' the archetypal inner steam of consciousness" (Anzaldúa, 2015, p. 98). El cenote is a deep well full of imagery, mystery, and creative power to be birthed. Like fertile soil, in darkness there is growth slowly pushing up, a new reality perturbing to the surface.

Anzaldúa explains the tension and 'pulling' between opposing realities as "suspended between traditional values and feminist ideas, [in which] you don't know whether to assimilate, separate, or isolate" (Anzaldúa, 2015, p. 126). In that nepantla moment, something seemingly essential to self-identity begins to shift; decolonization begins, an awareness to self and a pivotal place of agency and activism (Koshy, 2006). The despair and hopelessness experienced ushers into the next transformation, the Coatlicue state.

The Coatlicue state

Anzaldúa categorizes the Coatlicue state as the transformative act where we confront, head-on, the shadow beasts, the things inside of us that are buried deep and we would rather ignore or push aside. As one is in the Coatlicue state, you experience mictlán, the underworld. Despair is a site of sorrow and isolation; Anzaldúa situates the state of Coatlicue to an awareness of new knowledge as a form of resistance. In *Borderlands*, Anzaldúa (1999) describes the healing of the wounds, new knowledge, and resistance as the vision for a new mestiza. As Anzaldúa (1999) situated the wound as a visual, articulated metaphor for historical violence, psychological displacement, and a cry to recover the past and envision a new future, she illustrates the Coatlicue state through the lady of the serpent skirt (Vallone, 2014). It is where the creative self seeks time to resolve what they are going through in the process. Anzaldúa defines the Coatlicue state as: "represent[ing] the resistance to new knowledge and other psychic states triggered by intense inner struggle" (Anzaldúa, 2015, p. 242). Anzaldúa associates the Coatlicue state with a variety of situations, including depression, creativity, and writing blocks. These psychic conflicts are analogous to those she experiences as a Chicana. She explains the oppositional Mexican, Indian, and Anglo worldview she has internalized has led to self-division, cultural confusion, shame, and a wound (Anzaldúa, 2015). Anzaldúa references the Aztec symbol of Coatlicue, who, after being decapitated by her children, because they believed that she had committed unholy actions with a God, was saved by her unborn son Huitzlipochte who sprung from her womb as a warrior. Coatlicue felt great pain and sadness at her slain children despite their attempt on her life, and she made them the stars in the sky and her decapitated daughter, Coyolxauhqui, the moon.[6]

The Coatlicue state refers to Coatlicue, whom, "[a]ccording to Aztec mythic history, Coatlicue, is the earth goddess of life and death [;] and mother of the gods" (Anzaldúa, 2015, p. 242). Coatlicue is characterized by her creativity balancing her skulls, hearts, hands, and claws the duality of life and death, which connect her to the Earth deity Tlaltecuhtli, both consuming and regenerating life (Klein, 2008). Anzaldúa (1999) explains: "In her figure, all the symbols important to the religion and philosophy of the Aztecs are integrated" (p. 69). She further writes how Coatlicue is a prelude to the actual crossing to a 'new territory'. The new territory that Anzaldúa writes about is a form of

---

[6] Klein (2008) argues extensively that the "colossal statue of Coatlicue should be seen as a testament to her positive, life-giving abilities rather than her destructive powers" (p. 246).

attaining and producing knowledge. She explains, "Knowledge makes me more aware, it makes [me] more conscious. 'Knowing' is painful because after 'it' happens[.] I can't stay in the same place and be comfortable. I am no longer the same person I was before" (Anzaldúa, 1999, p. 70). In experiencing the transformative acts of the conocimiento process and autohistoria-teoría, curating facilitates a reconciling and/or re-framing of the past, present, and future in a myriad of new ways.

While surviving the trauma, susto, and inhabiting the fragmentation of nepantla, sinking into the underworld in the Coatlicue state is depleting. It is a time of denial, "shielding myself with ignorance" and sinking into depression (Anzaldúa, 2015, p. 130). After binging on mourning and grieving former life, Anzaldúa explains, I am ushered into the Coatlicue state, indulging in isolation. Anzaldúa explains: "You wallow in the ruins of your life—pobre de ti—until you can't stand the stench that's yourself" (Anzaldúa, 2015, p. 130). It is then that a new landscape can be taken in small doses. The evidence of new growth and understanding comes in little pockets pushing through fear and anxiety, forging a new reality. This transformation conocimiento transformative act is difficult because the patterns established throughout life are difficult to recognize and change; Anzaldúa writes, "habitual feelings [are] the hardest thing you've ever attempted" (Anzaldúa, 2015, p. 131).

Then, all of a sudden, "Coyolxauhqui's light (moon goddess) pulls me up, out of my grief" (Anzaldúa, 2015, p. 133). Coyolxauhqui supports and helps free me from my grieving because, by this transformational act, I also realize the depths of depression that I am in and want to heal. I want transformation, yet I still fight with resistance until I surrender and allow it all to happen, "[a]ll the lost pieces of myself come flying from the deserts and the mountains and the valleys, magnetized toward that center. Completa" (Anzaldúa, 1999, p. 73). I am made whole. A dying and being re-born of the self is a recurring action in the conocimiento process and necessary in engaging the healing process as the old self is left behind crossing thresholds into the self (Anzaldúa, 2015).

Reframing

The fourth transformation is a call to action of the self, a conscious knowledge that identity is fluid and change is not easy or neat, yet a choice needs to be made to engage in the healing process (Anzaldúa, 2015). The crossing may feel lonely because it can only be done by the crosser, but spiritual practice is part of this process, reminding the crosser of the interconnectedness to everything, "those of the invisible realm walk with you; there are ghosts on every bridge" (Anzaldúa, 2015, p. 137). It marks the leaving of one space (world) into another and redefining the self in who you are becoming—not who you were (Anzaldúa, 2015). Anzaldúa writes, "[t]he bridge (boundary between the world you've just left and the one ahead) is both a barrier and a point of transformation" as a continuous reinterpreting of the self and past is enacted reshaping the present (Anzaldúa, 2015, p. 137). The act of making a choice to cross and leave behind the old narratives and create new ones, a transformation in which the naguala/shapeshifter is actively at work (Zaytoun, 2015).

The calling of self to action that Anzaldúa delineates is our inner calling, our passions that motivate the self to imagine and create the life that exists within (Zaytoun, 2015). The price that needs to be paid repeatedly in this transformative act is the facing of the shadow beasts. Anzaldúa asks, "[a]re you sure you're ready to face the shadow beast guarding the threshold—that part of yourself holding your failures and inadequacies, the negatives you've internalized, and those aspects of gender and class you want to disown?" (Anzaldúa, 2015, p. 137).

This shift of leaving the old narratives behind and re-framing experiences is an intentional move as it takes so much energy, especially when you are already wounded and bleeding. Anzaldúa validates this struggle. She states: "[c]onocimiento hurts, but not as much as desconocimiento"[7] (Anzaldúa, 2015, p. 137). Listening and trusting the self is critical as curating our own's desires and passions; we also become contributing members of our communities, "one worthy of self-respect and love" (Anzaldúa, 2015, p. 136). Through active listening of self through the transformative conocimiento acts, we become fertile sites for new growth, transformation, putting ourselves together by curating intentional ways to re-envision self and create an autohistoria.

Autohistoria-teoría

Critically self-reflecting on both the past and present, perspectives change because every new angle offers a new way of envisioning and re-building self. Because historically underrepresented learners and educators/curators have been marginalized, absent from the academic canons, many times failing to see themselves within culture in positive, contributing ways in society. Often, marginalized groups are not realizing the coping mechanisms exercised daily to assimilate in an attempt to ease their feelings of not belonging.

Anzaldúa's approaches to several of her theories are derived from years of research and unpublished work about the naguala[8] or shapeshifting (Zaytoun, 2015). Anzaldúa's concept of the naguala is expansive, complicated, and dwells

---

[7] *Desconocimientos* is the Spanish word that Anzaldúa uses to describe both willed and unwilled ignorance. Epistemology of ignorance are the things we do not know and the things we do not want to know by choice.

[8] *Naguala* means shapeshifter in the Nahuatl language.

within conscious, unconscious, and spiritual worlds, realms, and forms that aren't exclusively material (Zaytoun, 2015). The entanglement of the naguala within Anzaldúa's theories is an important component because she expands what we (as individuals) are capable of if we channel the naguala, through imagination, as vessels where then creative acts are embodied, creating power to transform (Zaytoun, 2015). Anzaldúa explains that in making meaning for oneself via embodiment and creative acts, community is also affected by public acts initiating transformation through the conocimiento process. She uses her writing as an example illustrating how shapeshifting with her imagination, she is able to embody different experiences and then write about them, which in turn produces power to transform self and affect others (Anzaldúa, 2015; Zaytoun, 2015). Only when we send "our voices, visuals, and visions outward into the world, we alter the walls and make them a framework for new windows and door[s]" (Anzaldúa, 1990, p. xxv). Anzaldúa described this change-making as conocimiento, an initiator for critical reflective and consciousness work. She explains that conocimiento "is reached via creative acts—writing, art-making, dancing, healing, teaching, mediation, and spiritual activism—both mental and somatic (the body, too, is a form of, as well as site of, creativity)" (Anzaldúa, 2015, p. 119). The conocimiento process initiates critical consciousness work that connects to others because of the shapeshifting imagination that first flows through the self, creating inter-relatedness to others (Zaytoun, 2015). Critical consciousness and conocimiento processes are full of tensions and transformations, "allowing for transformative ruptures to occur" towards renewal (Gaxiola Serrano, Ybarra, & Delgado Bernal, 2019, p. 343).

Renewal

The sixth transformative act of conocimiento is to take the new story out into the world and test it. Taking our story that we have imagined, curated from fragments of our lived and historical experiences, out into the world and sharing it with others is extremely vulnerable, making our wounds exposed to the elements. In this vulnerability, the small fragments are about voice, re-constructing self after loss, and empowerment through intuition and spirituality. Through back and forth experiences, the yearning and void connect points that to embody a new story as we become the bridge. "Voyagers, there are no bridges, one builds them as one walks" (Anzaldúa, 2009, p. 243). Re-building a story with agency, not as a victim, but empowered is healing as new symbols for one's self are curated. Anzaldúa writes: "An image is a bridge between evoked emotion and conscious knowledge; words are the cables that hold up the bridge" (Anzaldúa, 2009, p. 121). Curating a new story and taking it into the world requires new consciousness and knowledge building through creative acts. For Anzaldúa, her creative acts manifested through words, writing, art, and building bridges to cross thresholds as a mediator, a nepantlera.

Nepantlera

In 1990, during the National Women's Studies Association (NWSA), a racist debate emerged, and Anzaldúa chose to remain and mediate as a neutral party after most women of color had walked out. Anzaldúa describes her embodied experience during the NWSA meeting of what a nepantlera could be in mediating an in-between space and becoming an active listener. Mediating by being an active listener is a feminist curatorial principle that is imperative in learner educative spaces. A mediator resides in-between, not choosing a side; she stands in the in-between space facilitating conversations (Koshy, 2015). It is in that moment of mediating that one becomes a nepantlera. The displacement and dislocation often experienced by nepantleras are integral in coming to terms with the discomfort and nomadic nature of mediation, that is, border crossing work. Anzaldúa created the term, nepantlera, and subsequently, her theory for nepantleras as a creator of holistic approaches towards reconciliation via creative acts (Anzaldúa, 2015). The nepantlera lives between worlds, under the bridge, existing simultaneously inside and outside the system. Keating describes an unaligned positionality as important in defining the nepantlera epistemology as a holistic way of knowing, which is based on similarities and connections, not on exclusions (Anzaldúa & Keating, 2009). Nepantleras are spiritual activists, searching for wholeness and deeper awareness (Anzaldúa, 1990). Becoming a nepantlera, a messenger that sees many perspectives in multiple contexts and acts, is what Kavitha Koshy (2006) terms nepantlera-activism.

As nepantleras, the educators, artists, and curators (the latter two also being educators) choose to mediate back and forth in the in-between spaces frequented, often transcultural ones (Koshy, 2006). A nepantlera means choosing not only to create and educate from a place of personal lived experiences but also to question who tells the stories, which stories and histories are told, and to whom, embodying the creative acts (Anzaldúa & Keating, 2009). The act of being a nepantlera transcends mere representation of self; it extends to the interconnectedness of cultural narratives.

Trans/national/cultural spaces

Similar to Zaytoun's (2015) description of classrooms as transitional spaces where border crossings, cross-cultural spaces and identities exist through multiplicitous entanglements, I am also positioning temporal homes as locations for possible exchanges for knowledge production. For example, transnational spaces may include the classroom space, artwork, or a curated gallery space. As creative acts occur, bridging is possible between people and experiences, allowing for healing through our wounds. As we heal from socially inflicted wounds of exclusion, we are able to take the fragments of our lived experiences and our creative acts to re-construct ourselves and re-make our identities. Anzaldúa (2002) and Zaytoun (2015) warn against alliances only made because of shared pain, often resulting in disempowering connections because of the emphasis on victim-hood and desconocimientos. I recognize the concerns as legitimate and important in mediating spaces as a nepantlera (a messenger) while curating, but the purpose is to help heal each other and self-empower. Autohistoria-teoría, through the conocimiento process, is relational, facilitating critical connections among diverse spaces and people towards transformation (Keating, 2006).

Underrepresented populations often feel a sense of not belonging in educational spaces because the reproduction of single narratives is often reproduced through resources, materials, and experiences highlighted and taught which are not diverse and fail to connect with students. When curating transcultural and transnational spaces, it is important to recognize the act of curating as a form of border crossing as a nepantlera. A curator, or curadora, is occupying multiple spaces critically while acknowledging fluid identities and cross-cultural politics with the aim towards new knowledge building, healing, and transformation through learning from one another (Koshy, 2006).

Fernando Ortiz first published the term transcultural in 1940 in discussing Cuban society and cultural exchanges between White and Black Cubans (Ortiz & Fernández, 1995). Although Ortiz's contribution of establishing a dialogue in the 1940s that would continue to resonate decades later is significant, it also has a very narrow and simplistic definition. Ortiz created the term transcultural in an attempt to highlight and bring awareness to the invisibility that Cuban culture, society, and government politics of the impact that the Black-Afro-Cuban had on White Cubans and vice-versa (Ortiz & Fernández, 1995). Unfortunately, Ortiz's term does not consider the complexities that are entangled within racial and cultural exchanges such as; socio-economic status, discrimination, gender, sexuality, oppressions, and historical contexts. For this reason, I borrow from Anzaldúa's more expansive definition of transcultural to mean multiple cultures intersecting in a given space or environment, including where multiple global issues, identities, cultures, or languages exist across national borders. A museum, classroom, or art gallery can serve as transcultural spaces where national borders are being crossed—physically, psychologically, and/or emotionally. The curadora has the power to omit or include knowledge or narratives to be shared, which vastly impact understandings of the world.

Reilly and Lippard (2018) explained the impact of Fred Wilson's 1992 exhibit, *Mining the Museum*, at the Maryland Historical Society, Baltimore, Maryland. They stated that Fred Wilson's 'telling' revealed an alternative historical account from the one narrated by the collection—one that underscored the fact that 'history' is necessarily a construction, an act of interpretation that gives rise to such questions as: How is history written? Whose history is being told?; Whose voice is silenced?; What role does a museum play in confirming hierarchies that value one culture or group over another? (p. 120)

The dominant colonizing narrative is frequently reinforced, which further oppresses underrepresented populations and excludes their experiences and historical contexts. In developing a process-oriented methodology, I introduced curating as integral to each transformative act of a conocimiento process as a way to decolonize the histories that dominate education. In developing a process-oriented feminist teaching approach and methodology, the goal is towards social change and justice. Through the conocimiento theory, curating is integral to each transformative act as a way to decolonize the histories of White patriarchy. Underrepresented people have wounds of exclusion or misrepresentation of their histories because of a colonizing narrative.

Colonialism, as Anzaldúa explains in an interview with Irene Lara, is the "act of invasion [, which] is a trauma, a wound which the whole country has not recovered from or attended to; it keeps bleeding in the psyches of Mexicans, Latinos, Blacks, Asians" (Keating, 2005, p. 54). I posit that healing such wounds as enacted through autohistoria-teoría and conocimiento as process-oriented feminist teaching infused in the curation of educational spaces is possible. Employing Anzaldúa's theories of autohistoria-teoría and conocimiento in curating course themes and syllabi provides a vocabulary and processes for transforming individual and collective voices through agency and knowledge building. Lugones's (2010) theory of decolonial feminisms unpacks the colonized lineage of Western understanding of gender, and therefore gender relations intersected with structures of oppression, which have impacted dominant understanding. She points out how Women of Color (WOC; e.g., Moraga & Anzaldúa, 2002; Ruth Behar, 1995; Chela Sandoval, 2013; Emma Pérez, 1999; Sylvia Marcos, 2009) have added new perspectives for writing histories about and for WOC that grapple multiplicitous realities and understandings in humanizing experiences of underrepresented people. This point is significant because I interpret Lugones's and Anzaldúa's theories of decolonization through history writing, testimonios, and embodying as disrupting dominant understanding of dichotomous thinking such as whole and fragmented. Instead of viewing wholeness/fragmented/broken binaries as pros/cons or right/wring, I choose to situate whole and fragmented as places for critical reflection of human conditions; individual, collective, broader issues to analyze. Curricular curation grapples with decentering binaries of whole/fragmented by critical reflecting on the complexities of underrepresented lived experiences.

By curating, I specifically reference both (a) intentional use of material centered in Anzaldúa's theories of autohistoria-teoría and conocimiento as facilitators within the classroom; and (b) student participation that occurs as I model and invite students to curate their own stories. Through the process of using a feminist, curated syllabus, students may experience the various stages of the seven transformative acts, ultimately creating the catalyst for reframing their own autohistoria.

In the first transformative act of rupture/fragmentation/fear, fear has often been historically used as an approach by the oppressor to limit, silence, and erase the voices of underrepresented populations in the United States. Critically reflecting, through writing and discussions of individualized internalization of these fears, experiences and the impact of larger issues that as underrepresented populations they grapple with at large. Conocimiento transformative acts involve nepantla, an in-between place of letting go of the old self, calling to action a nepantlera/crosser/visionary that reframes autohistorias into new collective stories of the world.

As students cross between transformative acts, they curate their own experiences of transformation, grappling with each one—transforming the past, present, and future narratives of their own lives. In my experience, as a student of color experiencing the transformative acts through my own grappling of hybrid identities (Puerto Rican-Cuban-American-ness) not fully knowing my own histories until later in life, I have chosen to cultivate my heritage and roots with a profound sense of ancestral connections that I did not have when living in desconocimientos (unknowing, consciously or unconsciously, ignorance).

Anzaldúa's (1999) theory of Borderlands situates the borderland as beyond the physical geographical borders of Mexico/United States. She expanded the concept of Borderland to include "psychic, sexual, and spiritual borderlands" (Anzaldúa, 2015, p. 242). Anzaldúa (1999) perceived living in a Borderland "in a state of psychic unrest" as the catalyst for creative acts (p. 95). These Borderlands also became sites for transformations, as "it was—and remains— a defining statement on the inextricability of sexuality, gender, race, and class for Chicana and changed the way we talk about the difference in sexuality, race/ethnicity, gender and class in the U.S." (Anzaldúa, 1999, p. 13). I apply Anzaldúa's conocimiento theory to curating as a psychic or spiritual crossing transcending physical borders to map the borders encompassing emotional, psychological, nostalgic and memory worlds. I define the use of the term world to refer to an individual or collective realm entered or created through a path of conocimiento. The world entered through the conocimiento pathway may be spiritual, psychological, emotional, physical, or abstract.

For example, my own heritage and ancestry are entangled within my Cuban, Puerto Rican, Spanish, Lebanese, and Taíno lineages, all of which are hyphenated with my Americanness, creating a sense of not belonging throughout my life. I align with Cuban-American writer and scholar Gustavo Pérez Firmat's (2012) theory of 'life on the hyphen/vidas en vilo,' where he builds on identities of children born abroad but educated and raised in the U.S as the one-and-a-half generation, focusing on this generation to emphasize its simultaneous adaptability to both cultures, inherited ideologies, and memory.

When underrepresented and underserved people use their personal histories in their work, their testimonio is revealed. Anzaldúa (1999) used the metaphor of a turtle carrying her home[9] with her wherever she goes to describe how underrepresented people carry their roots, heritage, and ancestry, as they navigate in-between spaces and cross borders. Experiencing the deep sense of not belonging so often felt by underrepresented students is integral for coming to terms with the uncomfortable and nomadic experiences of underrepresented people in higher education. As an educator curating curriculum, I facilitated the making or assembling of 'temporary homes' to use Anzaldúa's metaphor of the turtle, which become places that may enact a process for healing. As new narratives arise, these temporary homes become locations for education and decolonizing, for crossing borders that are emotional, psychological, nostalgic, historical, and memory-driven.

Healing

I began my professional journey by critically reflecting on my educational experiences from Preschool throughout my undergraduate career. For this reason, I begin with my autohistoria, my testimonio, as a location of personal lineage. The unpacking of myself through my testimonios radically began to reveal deep wounds and also eventually initiated the healing process. My historically low self-worth as a young woman grappling with college and relationships, having my native Spanish tongue shamefully reduced to private grunts, being thrown into different school environments and being forced to sink or swim—at any cost. In recognizing the wounds, pains, and coping skills that I endured throughout my education career, I was able to understand the coping skills and survival roles that I developed without knowing. I did not know the depth and pain of my wounds until my guard—my walls—began to

---

[9] In Taíno belief, we are descendants from a spiritual set of four male ancestors, Deminan Caracaracol, and a female spirit, Turtle Woman.

come down, until I entered nepantla. It was in nepantla that I began to understand the layers of my wounds, the scab that wouldn't heal. I use the term healing to delineate the intentionality of using this curatorial approach as a tool towards reconciling to ourselves, having empathy for each other, transforming into the best version of ourselves, embracing who we are at our cores unapologetically. For me, the term healing is synonymous with proactively creating our stories for ourselves, not identifying as others may want to—to intuitively honor and embody our beings without negotiating or compromising our voices.

Wounds may be caused by many things; society, culture, tradition, racism and systemic oppression, causing us to either recognize and be aware of something that was not visible prior or cause us to close up into ourselves and others (Anzaldúa, 2015). To choose to use pain "as a conduit to recognizing another's suffering, even that of the one who inflicted the pain" is a choice to enter into a spiritual practice. Anzaldúa explains healing of our wounds as a "spiritual practice of conocimiento"[10] that is a "port you moor to in all storms" (Anzaldúa, 2015, p. 154). Entering our wounds means vulnerability, but to stay in the wound as a victim is to allow desconocimiento,[11] a negative energy that is disempowering because it does not move towards transformation (Anzaldúa, 2015). However, by transforming our wounds through healing, they become strengths to "heal the traumas of racism and other systemic desconocimientos" (Anzaldúa, 2015, p. 154). To reach or heal through the wound is believing that aside from love, "pain might open this closed passage by reaching through the wound to connect" (Anzaldúa, 2015, p. 153).

Healing is an ongoing process of the soul, mind, spirit to focus all energy towards positivity and transformation, "[t]here is never any resolution, just the process of healing" (Anzaldúa, 2015, p. 20). Wounds provoke a longing for wholeness, a longing to feel and be connected to oneself and others completely. Anzaldúa explains, "healing as taking back the scattered energy and soul loss wrought by woundings" (Anzaldúa, 2015, p. 89). In taking back our energy, fragments, and pieces of ourselves, we work through the transformative acts of

---

[10] Anzaldúa (2015) states:
The spiritual practice of conocimiento, such as praying, breathing deeply, meditating, writing—dropping down into yourself, through the skin and muscles and tendons, down deep into the bones' marrow where your soul is ballast—enabled you to defuse the negative energy of putdowns, complaints, excessive talk, and verbal attacks, as well as other killers of the spirit. (p. 154).

[11] Desconocimiento as an act is defined by Anzaldúa as "[s]mall acts of desconocimientos ignorance, frustrations, tendencies toward self-destructiveness, feelings of betrayal and powerlessness, and poverty of spirit and imagination" (Anzaldúa, 2015, p. 154).

conocimiento in the strive and struggle to put ourselves back together. We embrace, sit, resist, and challenge our pain, our wounds. We touch them, pick at them—let them scab over—they bleed, are sutured up—again. It is in conocimiento's recursiveness that we are continuously dying to self and being reborn, taking our fragmented parts and, like Coatlicue, resurrecting. But as we rebuild ourselves, we are not putting ourselves together in the way we were once before, but because we have transformed through the process, we are different. Our shape has changed because we have changed. In the rebuilding, we take the fragments that have changed through conocimiento and rebuild ourselves in a new way. Anzaldúa explains that conocimiento and autohistoria-teoría are catalysts for new paths to be forged through theoretical work, ways of understanding, creating knowledge, and awareness, and I posit that conocimiento and autohistoria-teoría initiate a rebuilding of oneself in a new way, differently. By curating educational spaces and allowing for lived experiences to connect with others and historical and relevant contexts, active theorizing emerges, creating new pools of knowledge. As one of the transformative acts of the conocimiento process, Anzaldúa invokes Coyolxauhqui as a symbol of the "ongoing process of making and unmaking" and "putting the pieces together in a new way" (Anzaldúa, 2015, p. 20).

Healing through our wounds is for our individual selves, our community, and "to begin to heal the world" (Anzaldúa, 2015, p. 21). By changing the narratives that exist through our own pain, we embody new positive life-changing beliefs. Healing empowers us to "share strategies on peaceful coexistence" and conocimiento through compassion and empathy, enabling us to "extend our hand to others con el corazón con razón en la mano" (Anzaldúa, 2015, p. 20). As I critically reflected on my experiences as a student and educator and what I had witnessed with my students' engagement, I was mining for overall sentiments of feelings that emerged, such as gratitude, empathy, struggles, connections, depth, and understanding. Words alone, I realized, are not enough in this analysis of the process of transformational learning because transformation is a matter of the heart, soul—our spirit— but at some point, a manifestation of this comes out through creative acts. A holistic lens for transformative learning to notice the larger picture, a process perhaps in action.

Curadora/Curator

Reframing and naming life narratives is an act of germinating a vision, a conjuring of one's self, one created by sowing the ignored seeds into stories of empowerment. Because minority or underrepresented life stories are not part of dominant culture discourse, underrepresented people feel a strong sense of not belonging. It is possible for curators and learners to change their experience of historical devaluation and sense of not belonging. My thesis is that the empowerment of reconciling one's whole self is possible through conocimiento and autohistoria-teoría as a form of curando[12]—healing. The role of curadora/curator as a holistic practice includes the intersections of artist, curator, educator, researcher, scholar, everyday humanness as recognizing the *whole* Self. Rita Irwin (2006) discusses a/r/tography as a place to curiously inquire as learners and educators, as a place of understanding as a process, not a resolution. I draw a parallel here between practice-based research in art education and an approach to curating as a form of re-searching. I juxtapose Anzaldúa's (2015) theories of autohistoria-teoría and conocimiento as a path for inquiry of in-between spaces through practice-based research. I layer Emma Pérez's decolonial imaginary (1999) in two ways: by intentionally recognizing the in-between spaces as opportunities for new perspectives and re-imagining the margins as a place for empowerment and embodied decolonizing. In other words, I am defining curating as a way to decolonize through embodiment (lived/everyday experiences/testimonio), re-imagining and re-searching (histories, stories, new ways of envisioning), and choosing/creating our narratives—autohistorias as we see fit for ourselves. I refer to this concept as a form of curando/curating because, in the same way that one would curate an art exhibit or create artworks in the studio, we choose how to frame, write, dictate and embody our autohistorias and how to theorize them for ourselves while resisting/challenging how we may have been told to construct them.

I am also highlighting the word curadora/curator in its Spanish meaning tied to curando—or healing as the process of healing, not about the final product but the process of going into our wounds, pain, discomfort, and intentionally healing ourselves as curators. Let us be clear, the excavating and vulnerability that curating demands as a holistic approach through autohistoria-teoría also expands beyond binary boundaries into spiritual realms and collective healing as a form of activism (Bhattacharya & Keating, 2018). Autohistoria is a suturing of the Self through the process of curating, and henceforth I use this concept as the basis for curriculum curation as a nepantlera, a messenger that intentionally and simultaneously is within and outside using Anzaldúa's conceptualization of autohistoria-teoría actively to curate fragmented stories and creative acts via personal and professional spaces in academia (Bhattacharya & Keating, 2018; Anzaldúa, 2015). Kakali Bhattacharya and Rachél Paine (2016) offer an example of autohistoria-teoría through a collaboration with a friend and licensed counselor to create art and reflective writing as an embodied piece of work revisiting her experiences as a woman of

---

[12] Curando is the Spanish word for healing.

color in higher education and themes of exile, belonging and pain. Similarly, I have modeled a back-and-forth dialogue between learners and my facilitation in the classroom environment while investigating power dynamics and interrogating similarities versus differences from the liminal, in-between space nepantla.

The *Latina Feminisms* course focused on the process rather than the end results. For example, the process of healing is ongoing and fluid—individual and collective as we (educator and learner) share our vulnerabilities, wounds, and lived experiences; we begin to recognize our interconnectedness. The journey of critical self-reflection, transformation, and the process of healing are all interwoven and implicit within one another. Anzaldúa's theory of conocimiento advocates for consciousness and living with full awareness of our realities while creating our autohistorias (Anzaldúa, 2015).

I also expand and push the teacher inquiry process through a feminist and transformative position for both the learner and the educator/curator. An inclusive approach expands teaching transformations to include interconnectedness through our similarities; economically, ecologically, linguistically, spiritually, and socially. Keating describes selfhood as "permeable"; not that differences are ignored, but rather contextualized and interconnectedness is expanded because of what we have in common and may learn and grow; transforming (Keating, 2007, p. 10). A feminist teacher inquiry process working towards transformation for all involved (teacher culture, educator, students, institutions, etc.) is part of spiritual activism—where visions are enacted—thus serving as a model for others. Anzaldúa stated, "the ability to recognize and endow meaning to daily experience (spirituality) further[s] the ability to shift and transform" (Moraga & Anzaldúa, 2002, p. 568). In other words, through nepantla, a transitioning/birthing process, a nepantlera comes into existence, a boundary crosser among many worlds, tapping into a connectionist faculty (Keating, 2005).

Anzaldúa names la facultad as an inner psychic, knowing is practiced with daily rituals from indigenous communities or curanderas,[13] like chamanas,[14] artists, spiritual activists and nepantleras. Anzaldúa describes curanderas as "liminal people, at the thresholds of form, forever betwixt and between" (Anzaldúa, 2015, p. 31). For curanderas, realities shift. Curanderas are able to travel to other worlds inhabiting spiritual and physical realms that often are "unseen by those whose awareness focuses entirely on the ordinary reality of

---

[13] Curandera is the Spanish word for healer who uses folk medicines.
[14] Chamana is the feminine in Spanish of shaman that Anzaldúa uses throughout her writings. (Anzaldúa, 2015, p. 223).

daily life" (Anzaldúa, 2015, p. 32). Curanderas, for example, may use material objects, prayers, specific mantras, or phrases mingled with anything from nature to herbs in the process of healing a person and restoring a soul or spirit. The back and forth crossings for a chamana or curandera is the "method of deriving knowledge and power to perform these activities" (Anzaldúa, 2015, p. 33). As the back and forth crossings into various transformative acts in the conocimiento process, the chamanería[15] journey is a tearing and re-constructing "incorporating a wider vision" (Anzaldúa, 2015, p. 33).

Curanderismo are traditional healers, a spiritual practice carried through cultural lineages through a holistic practice of the mind, body, and soul. According to Aztec ritual practices, for example, Coatlicue and other female deities were often consulted and honored for their "extraordinary generative powers" (Klein, 2008, p. 243). In a similar way, I situate curadora/curator as a type of healer or a facilitator of a healing process that requires a back and forth crossing into other realms, much like a nepantlera. As an underrepresented educator, artist, writer (creative acts), I/we are constantly border crossing, as a messenger. Through Anzaldúa's theories of conocimiento and autohistoria-teoría, I situate curadora/curator as a healer, emphasizing the curatorial practice through creative acts towards healing and transformations. In the process of the back and forth border crossing, the educator and the learner, I believe, can intentionally set to suture themselves and their interactions as places for healing.

Using Anzaldúa's theories of autohistoria-teoría and conocimiento for curating art educational spaces provided a method to address learners' deep sense of not belonging. Curating educational spaces bear the possibility of transformation and healing because la curadora, the healer, is creating or conjuring an environment that is intentional in facilitating dialogues, curiosities, and for learners to engage as they are. In other words, a curator conjures up, earnestly, into existence a new or different perspective.

A connectionist faculty, Anzaldúa explains, means to fluidly engage in a creative re-imagining of unifying points rather than staunch divisions. Anzaldúa's connectionist theory blurs the boundaries of difference by focusing on the

---

[15] Chamanería is the Spanish word used to describe shamanism as a system of healing through spiritual practice that is "more than forty thousand years old "(Anzaldúa, 2015, p. 223). Additionally, Anzaldúa clarifies that
Shamanism" is an invention of Western anthropologists. The word "shaman" originated with the Tungus tribe of Siberia. A Shaman is "one who sees in the dark" and has the ability to see 'with the strong eye,' or to travel to the hidden sprit worlds to find information and to preform acts that will heal a person or the community. (Anzaldúa, 2015, p. 223)

similarities that connect individuals. Curating educational spaces makes accessible the connections that may not otherwise coincide, allowing opportunities for healing. Healing is facilitated by the curadora, who is also a nepantlera, a crosser, a mediator in the educational space, offering perspectives and creating new perspectives with learners. The nepantlera, the educator, must have an intentional mindset and spiritual practice for self-realization. By self-realization, I mean to be self-reflective and engaging within a transformation process as part of a lived (spiritual) practice. Of course, this may take a variety of limitless forms, which I have defined for myself as curatorial pillars of call for awakening, vulnerability to self and others, wandering/sense of not-belonging, healing, and interconnectedness. The curatorial pillars that have emerged for me arise from my testimonio, what I have experienced in my life in general and specifically as a learner and educator. But it also has everything to do with my spiritual journey of Self as the place for learning and growth connected to mind, body and spirit. In this way, curating educational environments are spaces for holistic spiritual engagement as whole people. This is an important point in how we see each other. We see each other as broken individuals, who are damaged, instead of seeing each other as whole beings who are transforming, as places to share and connect in the spiritual and knowledge growth.

Curatorial educational environments can be deeply intimate, vulnerable spaces for interconnectedness. New ways of learning and knowledge are created by inscribing various forms, creativity/creative acts. What curating educational spaces do not entail is a regurgitation of information, a traditional banking system of education (Freire, 1970; Mendez-Negrete, 2013). It does not support a monologue but rather conversations with the creative acts through individual and collective lived experiences, histories, and various contexts.

Often, the academic canon is only focusing on over-represented dominant White male canons, like the Banyan tree, completely isolated and removed from all other roots (Anzaldúa, 1999). As curadora (healer, curator), I curate with the intention of holistic learning to be created together in educational spaces. For the creative acts to activate healing, the individual works through the transformative acts of conocimiento for *themselves* rather than from the outside-in as a third person (Anzaldúa, 2015). Again, I am reminded of the connection between the Banyan wasps and the curating of new perspectives and academic canons as pollinating and germinating seeds towards transformations from the inside. Curating educational spaces facilitates the creative acts as possible new healing and connectionist theories because the curation considers a holistic framework of the mind, body, spirit, and soul. Like Anzaldúa's imagery of curanderismo, "indigenous healing practice or shamanism, mixed with beliefs, rituals, and specific practices, and the shamanic journey where one is able to shape shift (in Náhuatl, nagual) and travel to other realities" I want to mirror through curating (Anzaldúa, 2015, p. 215). Anzaldúa explains that the role of the shaman (often also considered a poet) is "to preserve and create cultural or group identity by mediating between the cultural heritage of the past and the present everyday situations people find themselves in" (Anzaldúa, 2009, p. 121). Transformation is a matter of the heart; it is not something that can be measured within the classroom experience. Similar to the Banyan tree wasps that germinate from within, producing a fruit that holds a blooming flower within it, transformation is an ongoing process that grows internally, producing fruit outwardly.

I posit that creative acts, critical self-reflection, and collaborative efforts occur within the classroom, studio, and gallery spaces as temporary transnational spaces that become vulnerable through our lived experiences and theorizing about our experiences. I situate transnational spaces as places where nepantleras intentionally situate the Self within and work towards transforming transnational spaces into collaborative critically-reflective environments while also occupying various standpoints and spaces while engaging critically within them. In turn, these transnational spaces become sites for nepantlando, the term I use to signal nepantla as activation.[16] As curators and/or nepantleras in various environments, we are mediators, finding commonalities and meaningful dialogues (Zaytoun, 2015). Conocimiento is a transformation process, healing process, and critical self-awareness; it is a form of resistance and spiritual activism. The power of creative acts is a manifestation of spiritual activism, enabling new perspectives to come about, to reimagine and reconstruct, exposing layers and realities that did not exist before (Keating, 2005).

---

[16] Nepantlando: My collaboration and work with Dr. Christen Sperry García is developing a theoretical conceptual framework using Gloria Anzaldúa's theory of conocimiento and nepantlera whereas educators and artists we situate a third space of nepantlando as an activated place for the back and forth border crossings we engage in and with our students.

Chapter 3

Decolonial feminist thoughts

I have struggled to find an adequate word in discussing decolonization and decentering because of their over-use, especially in academia. Most notably, the word decolonize is often used interchangeably with efforts towards social justice, change, diversity, multiculturalism, and race relations. To decenter something to me means that I am intentionally interrupting a pattern that is in existence and changing the focus in some way. The Merriam-Webster dictionary defines decenter as: to cause to lose or shift from an established center or focus; disconnecting from practical or theoretical assumptions. I use the word decolonize to mean that the U.S. public education system has historically supported colonialism and the imposition of Eurocentric values, norms, and modes of thinking about other people, countries, culture, traditions, languages and overall customs; causing psychological trauma and misunderstanding in others that fall outside of a Eurocentric context (Creary, 2012).

Latina feminisms and decolonial feminisms: Genealogies and overviews

Latin American and Latinx contexts have reshaped the thinking of mainstream thinking in regard to the decolonial development and arguments, as philosophers have questioned the inextricable entanglements of colonial structures and categorial logic (Velez & Tuana, 2020). Raewyn Connell (2014) asserts that theories from the global north are generally universally accepted while southern theory is often labeled according to its geographical place of origins suggesting that global southern theories are only to be applied to particular geographic spaces. Connell also argues that the scholarship is dependent on a few "celebrity" authors predominantly from the North writing in globally dominant languages. Jean and John Comaroff (2015) explain how often knowledge production comes from the global North while data is provided by the global South. Ngũgĩ' wa Thiong'o's (1998) book, *Decolonizing the Mind*, expands the conversation by analyzing the effects of imperialism as leaving its imprint on the minds of the previously colonized, causing a detachment from their immediate surroundings and culture in order to personalize what was once different and far off. Maria Lugones (2010) explains striving towards feminism that is decolonized by analyzing the power dynamics between colonized and colonizer and the intersectionality of race, gender, and sexuality.

Decolonization is a process that requires time and is filled with complex questioning. Who or what determines when decolonization occurs? How is decolonization occurring? Decentering is also a process-oriented term; however, to me, it offers more possibility to take action in the now. For example, because my research work is about and in the curating of curriculum, to can employ a decentering approach in my teaching, facilitating, and materials and resources readily. However, the same cannot be said about decolonizing—instead, to decolonize—is an ongoing process beyond a curriculum and classroom experience as it impacts invisible areas of the human experiences such as: perspectives of self and others, the everyday walk in life, interactions, and critical self-reflections and questioning of the world as inhabited daily. Both terms are limiting and important. I am tempted to create terminology that combines them both: de/center/coloniz/ing.

Della Pollock (1998) explains the act of "performing writing" in Feminist performative writing is: provocative, metonymic, subjective, nervous, (re)citational, and consequential. According to Pollock, writing is both to create meaning and make writing a meaningful process. Writing, especially feminist performative writing, is a struggle full of restlessness—a process of deep, critical introspectiveness that is an embodiment of the soul in textual form. A spiritual encounter that one must delve deep into the self. Tara Lockhart (2006) explains that writing, as shown through Anzaldúa's (1999) *Borderland* book, is not only "a way of doing or of communicating, but a way of oscillating between ways of understanding, making meaning, and interpreting" (Lockhart, 2006, p. 107). Theorist Louise Rosenblatt has noted that the process of meaning-making through writing is an enactment between the reader, test, and by extension, the writers (Rosenblatt & Booth, 1995). Anzaldúa repeatedly comes back to the idea of our stories, testimonios, autohistorias as performances. She parallels the performance of writing to art works/making—a collaborative effort between the reader and writer, or artist. In other words, feminist performative writing is an act of creativity—an embodiment of the self through text. I define feminist performative writing as a method of decolonizing the self and knowledge, by activating our (my) autohistoria-teoría through testimonios.

Terminology: Decolonization and decolonial feminisms

The word decolonizing is charged with a tone of activism that seems to be popular in current day research and scholarly work under this label—decolonizing as a concept of undoing something—that was so negative that it permeated every part of life. A stain that cannot be fully washed out. Many words come to mind in the fight against colonization; imperialism, land, colonies, slave/master narratives, etc. But what do I mean by decolonizing? Decolonizing a curriculum? Or the process of decolonizing?

Raymond Betts (2012) explains the global historical overview of the decolonization process getting traction after World War II that would run rapidly for the next three decades. But this was only one specific definition of decolonization; a political one (Betts, 2012). From a politicized concept of decolonization, recognition of other components or forms of society were affected by colonization that was also oppressive, such as economic, cultural, mind/intellectual, and metropoles (Betts, 2012). Anzaldúa, in her *Borderland* theory (1999), explains colonization through the visceral descriptors of una herida abierta (an open wound) that not only centers on manmade borders but also psychic unrest that affects all of a person. Furthermore, decolonization is not an all-encompassing process, and the effects of colonialism run deep. Colonization, historically, was a process, not a moment in time. Subsequently, decolonization is a process that requires time to dismantle. However, do I/we need to use the term decolonizing in order to be doing decolonization? I struggle to use this popular trending term in my work because of all of the baggage *it* comes with—the box that my work may be put into because of *it*. However, I have not yet come to a better term for the action/intention/purpose of de-colonizing—the process of renewing one's self to unlearn many of the oppressive things that I've learned. This does not mean that I do not encounter colonizing perceptions, power dynamics, institutions, or even work within colonized environments, but it does mean that I am intentional through my autohistoria-teoria, my everyday practice, not to perpetuate binaries and power dynamics that are demeaning, hierarchal, oppressive, and silencing.

Decolonial imaginary

In her groundbreaking text, *The Decolonial Imaginary: Writing Chicanas into History* (1999), Emma Pérez advocates for the necessity of interrogating what she calls the "colonial imaginary" that has circumscribed hegemonic regimes of power. She posits that through decolonizing the imaginary, we find opportunities to decolonize identities, histories and epistemologies towards a reconceptualization of a decolonized feminist praxis. Pérez develops the concept of the decolonial imaginary as resistance to the colonial imaginary that has determined what counts as historical knowledge in academic spaces, particularly claiming that history is an objective science (1999, xiv-xvi). Challenging objective and universalist conceptions of history by highlighting the partiality and fragmentation of historical narratives and archives, she argues, "There is no pure, authentic, original history. There are only stories—many stories" (1999, xv). Furthermore, I conversely situate testimonios, lived experiences, as valid places for knowledge building within the classroom environment, which explicitly decanters the traditional thinking of expertise/genius that permeates academic thinking. Within the in-between spaces, an alternative is created for rewriting our autohistorias as active curators of the Self. This, I believe, must not be taken for granted because repeatedly, I witness the possibility of seeing ourselves and each other in new ways when we travel through our experiences and engage with theorizing of the self; autohistoria-teoría. Emma Velez (2019) unpacks her own journey as an educator in the classroom with Latina students traveling through uncomfortable yet embodied spaces of decoloniality that are necessary to challenge the traditional narratives and histories curated to silence keep us out.

In turn, decolonizing the imaginary pushes forth a rupturing that resonates with Anzaldúa's positionality of nepantla, an in-between space that resists and challenges the linear process often imposed by colonialism. Furthermore, the rupturing that occurs within in-between spaces occurs within the oppressive systems that they are born from, further unpacking what Anzaldúa discusses as desconocimientos; willed ignorance or things unknown. The awareness and going into the wound (Anzaldúa, 2015) is the catalyst for exposing the desconocimientos once recognized, witnessed, and resisting histories and dismantling aspects of colonially.

Chapter 4

Borderland theory in curating a *Latina Feminisms* curriculum

I noticed that in my classes, several feelings rose to the surface from my students and myself: curiosity, pain, trauma, violence, frustration, vulnerability, awakening, storytelling, disempowerment, exhaustion, identities, reclaiming of self (in need of, not knowing how, or coming to terms of), expansion of perspectives and interconnectedness. Feminist teacher inquiry of my experiences teaching the undergraduate course *Latina Feminisms, Latinas in the US: Gender, Culture and Society* to form the theoretical framework to curate the syllabus, but also to assess my teaching toward student critical self-reflection and listening, self-empowerment, and healing. I have critically reflected on my experiences and observed my students all as part of my theorizing process, specifically noting the markers that have emerged as a result of the journeying together. This chapter is organized in four sections on the research methodologies of (a) researcher positionality, (b) a feminist teacher inquiry process, (c) analysis approach, and (d) self-theorizing.

Primary data sources include field notes, observations, conference meetings with students, and journal reflections. Secondary data sources include student work as artifacts, anonymous surveys, class assignments, discussions, and student journal reflections. Curating the curriculum for the *Latina Feminism* course began by considering what type of environment I wanted to help create with others. I emphasize here the co-creating component. Transformative learning cannot occur without a 'we' mentality; we share the space, we are impacted by each other, we learn from each other, we build together. Co-creating includes the educator and the learner; because I aim to have as minimal a hierarchal structure as possible, in my educative spaces, co-creating is crucial. We can co-create by facilitating meaningful conversations that dive deep, with no judgments, respectability and caring as whole people.

I explicitly challenge the traditional notions of mechanical education by inviting learners to hone in on their own knowledge and creative acts and instigating 'pollination' from within themselves. The purpose of class sharing is for students and learners to recognize that although we all have different personal stories, wounds, and backgrounds, we are all interconnected somehow. By actively listening to each other, we can develop empathy and *initiate a process of healing for ourselves* as individuals but also as a collective through vulnerability and intimacy. The very act of writing within "suppressed knowledge" and "marginalization" is an embodied practice of decolonizing. I found that as a feminist facilitator, I must be on my own journey of self-awareness, consciousness, self-empowered, and a critical self-reflective person. The key difference is significant: writing *about* decolonization and writing *within* decolonization are two very different acts, which impact different results. Writing about *something* is informational, self-help of sorts, a guide to structuring something fixed that is replicable. But writing *within* is an approach and action that will vary depending on individuals and their experiences. It is not fixed but fluid. Writing *within* is a way to *approach* a situation that directly impacts or influences the individual—not advice or steps but a way of *doing*. For example, much research has been executed on the ideas post-1980s about multiculturalism and diversity and its integration into the curriculum. Lucy Lippard (1990), Andrea O'Reilly Herrera (2011), Reilly (2017), Desai (2019), and many others have established that there is a blatant difference between incorporating diversity as a recipe for color versus an actual integration of diversity. Anzaldúa stretches this even further by explaining that the actual doing within these curricular landscapes and boundaries is an embodiment of the experience and work of decolonizing. Anzaldúa, for example, did not only write about marginalized experiences; she wrote from *within* them.

I situate non-oppositional politics by initiating conversations and reflective points that offer two significant pieces. First, unpacking how historically, we (as learners) have been conditioned to understand others and ourselves through an oppositional perspective and in relation to Whiteness. Secondly, I challenge curiously with new perspectives in order to not reproduce oppositional politics but rather question and inspire social change as an active listener. By active listeners, I mean action and critical self-reflectiveness as collective laborers in the shared space. Learners and I unpacked the dangers of binaries with the working assumption that we are all biased while critically self-reflecting on our own lived experiences. For example, three students who identified as Latina/o and/or Hispanic struggled with traditional binaries and labeling their identities in the U.S. and their ancestral countries. As we (as a class) tried to define what we mean by Latina/o, it became difficult because of the entanglements to race, ethnicity, heritage, language, and culture. These three students, and as a class, we grappled with questions such as:

I do not speak Spanish fluently; can I identify as Latinx?[1] My family has assimilated into English American culture and society, I have little heritage to connect to, how does this impact my identity? How am I able to honor both identities I embody? My grandparent is the last remaining connection I have to my heritage and culture, how may I preserve them and their impact on my life? I am constantly crossing between my English American world and my Spanish speaking Mexican/Peruvian/Caribbean worlds—I do not fit into either one completely, how do I negotiate this? Conversely, students who identified as White American grappled with questions of: How has my Mennonite family and culture I grew up in impact my identity? Now that I realize the layers of silencing that have historically occurred in the U.S. I feel rage and shame—what do I do with this? How am I being held accountable for our history? How am I responsible? Benefiting? Where is my privilege in all of this?

Learners and I critically questioned if and how individual and collective change can be possible without using identity-based distinctions as a weapon against each other.

Over the course of the semester, we returned to the questions raised by students at our first few class sessions: How do I identity? Culturally? Ethnically? Have I felt marginalized? When? Why? What are my experiences so far in life? What do I know about my own history? Why haven't I had a class like this before? Trying to unpack and critically analyze and self-reflect on these questions, curiously, the possibilities of knowing our own histories and being valued and supported through our educational careers.

My conceptual framework for both the curriculum and my teaching, birthed from my autohistoria-teoría testimonio and Anzaldúa's theories of autohistoria and conocimiento, formed the parameters in which I structured my syllabus. In curating a *Latina Feminisms* syllabus, I had certain points in mind that I wanted to be sure to address in a class that had not been taught at the Pennsylvania State University for more than eight years. I was also mindful of my physical embodiment in the classroom as a Latina and Feminist, as I do not attempt to conceal some of my identities, such as ethnicity and standpoint. For many students who have experienced similarities to my own, I was the first Latina they have met who is pursuing a graduate school, pursuing a doctorate degree and teaching a *Latina Feminisms* course, which is their first undergraduate course in this subject area. My physical positionally in a predominantly White institution is significant because, in many ways, I am

---

[1] Latinx: relating to, or marked by Latin American heritage —used as a gender-neutral alternative to *Latino* or *Latina (Merriam-Webster, retrieved on February 23, 2020).*

representing a historical context that many learners know very little about. By engaging learners to become aware of their own privilege and power, I hope we/students will reflect on their ignorance and separation from their own roots due to colonialism and a White supremacist education. For this reason, I am intentional about discussing the entanglements of our identities as multiple and complex—my aim, in facilitating and guiding conversations within the course is a collective journey is not one to find answers but rather to dig deep into ourselves in an effort towards empathy, transformation, and the process of healing.

Researcher positionality: Teaching toward transformative learning with non-oppositional politics

Through the curating of the course, *Latina Feminisms*, I was curious how not belonging could emerge for myself and my students. In my critical self-reflections throughout the transformative acts of conocimiento in the past, I have been able to articulate many of my feelings of not belonging as intersected with many components of my identity and lived experiences. However, walking into the first week of the semester to teach *Latina Feminisms*, a course that I had taught the previous year twice, I assumed that I would be walking into, as years prior, Latina/o majority of students. To my surprise, it wasn't. In fact, I only had three students that self-identified as Latina/o/Hispanic out of the ten total students. My immediate concerns were some bursts of thoughts like:

> *Do I need to re-write my syllabus now since the majority of my students are non-Latina/o identifying? How will they read me, a Latina instructor?*

But, the thoughts passed through as I laughed at the irony of the situation—what better way to implement my research, which has a basis of interconnectedness, not belonging, and non-oppositional politics, than with students that I am assuming may have little common ground to each other, or me. My intentions for non-oppositional politics within my curation practice is to create an environment, a space, an energy that contributes to financing our similarities and pivoting critical reflection and analysis as a place for examining our human conditions, not to pivot ourselves against each other. This is important to me to begin from a non-oppositional praxis towards transformation and healing rather than focusing on our opposing stances that may exist.

I dove into the materials and class as planned with much curiosity about how the semester would go. Three out of the ten students were exchange students from London, studying a year abroad for their major in American Studies. They explained that there aren't many classes, if any at all, on Latin America or the Caribbean in London; hence, they were very excited to take the class. Some of the students, myself included, chuckled because it seems there are few classes or programs on Latin America at universities in the United States.[2]

A feminist teacher inquiry process working towards transformation for all involved (teacher culture, educator, students, institutions, etc.) is part of spiritual activism—where visions are enacted—thus serving as a model for others (Keating, 2005). Anzaldúa stated, "the ability to recognize and endow meaning to daily experience (spirituality) further[s] the ability to shift and transform" (Moraga & Anzaldúa, 2002, p. 568). In other words, through nepantla, a transitioning/birthing process, a nepantlera comes into existence, a boundary crosser among many worlds, tapping into a connectionist faculty (Keating, 2005).

A nepantlera builds towards "lifelong efforts to develop inclusionary multicultural alliances for social justice" (Keating, 2005, p. 2). Bridging Anzaldúa's theory of las nepantleras with her theories— of conocimiento and autohistoria-teoría as a form of moving towards self and collective healing through our wounds[3]—can create spiritual activism. I position the educator/teacher as curator/curadora; the healer, facilitating conversations into acts of conocimiento (Anzaldúa, 2015).

I also borrow from Keating's (2007) theory of teaching transformations to expand and push the teacher inquiry process through a feminist and transformative position for both the learner and the educator/curator. A multicultural approach in teaching transformations includes interconnectedness through our similarities; economically, ecologically, linguistically, spiritually, and socially (Keating, 2007). Keating describes selfhood as "permeable"— not that differences are ignored, but rather contextualized and interconnectedness is expanded because of what we have in common and may learn and grow—transforming (Keating, 2007, p. 10).

Anzaldúa's theory of conocimiento advocates for consciousness and living with full awareness of our realities while creating our autohistorias (Anzaldúa, 2015). In facilitating the *Latina Feminisms* class, I emphasized critical self-reflection as a mode for learners to take inventory of their own lived experiences and feelings throughout the semester as they recorded their insights on their personal blogs.

The *Latina Feminisms* course focused on the process rather than the end results. For example, the process of healing is ongoing and fluid—individual and collective as we (educator and learner) share our vulnerabilities, wounds, and lived experiences; we begin to recognize our interconnectedness. The

---

[2] A list of universities in the U.S. with Latin American programs is at http://lanic.utexas.edu/la/region/las-org/

[3] Healing is an ongoing process that never ends.

journey of critical self-reflection, transformation, and the process of healing are all interwoven and implicit within one another.

A feminist teacher inquiry process

In order to research a process-oriented feminist teaching methodology, I turned to practitioner inquiries, action research, and reflective practitioner scholarship to design my study. Teacher inquiry processes involve the systematic, intentional study of one's own professional practice to challenge assumptions about teacher and learning and knowledge (Dana & Yendol-Hoppey, 2014, p. xiv). Furthermore, teacher inquiry processes are intentional strategies toward goals of education reform and transforming understandings of knowledge (Dana & Yendol-Hoppey, 2014). Employing a feminist methodology in the teacher inquiry process provides a space for me to transform and grow as an educator, curator, researcher, and learner with "goals to build agency, empowerment ... and transformative characteristics" (Keifer-Boyd, 2014, p. 193). A feminist teacher inquiry framework is defined by transformative foundational components for exposing and critiquing the goal for social change, empowerment, connecting my individual narrative to collective stories, and building new paths. The feminist teacher inquiry approach and the theory of conocimiento are both akin to the transformative symbol of the spiral; the beginning and end do not exist. Through the spiral path of conocimiento, the traumas, struggles, differences, and contradictions are able to transform and connect to spiritual activism, creating communities that can imagine new realities and work together. My goal in curating a feminist teacher inquiry approach for transformative learning is to effect social change.

Applying a feminist teacher inquiry approach for the *Latina Feminisms* undergraduate course meant that I, too, learn and evolve throughout the semester with my students. I curated the syllabus situating Anzaldúa's (1999) pioneering book, *Borderlands,* as the required foundational text manifesting her theories of autohistoria-teoría and conocimiento. Anzaldúa's *Borderlands* is an example of autohistoria, and through my interpretation of the book chapters, I guided students on a journey through the seven transformative acts of the conocimiento process. I also chose the book because it is an example of a creative act as Anzaldúa interjects the poetic process in conveying her theories. The *Latina Feminisms* course syllabus is organized with the seven transformative acts of conocimiento as themes throughout the 15-week course. Each transformative act is explored along with *Borderlands* and supplemental materials, including additional readings authored by other scholars and educators who discuss Anzaldúa's seven transformative acts of conocimiento, films, poetry, and creative arts to help clarify or broaden chapters in *Borderlands* (Anzaldúa, 1999).

Despite having a syllabus that had been carefully curated, it was only a beginning plan and would allow the curriculum to unfold organically. By allowing the curriculum to unfold as needed in the classroom, I challenge and resist academia's top-down depository of information educational model. I facilitated a feminist inquiry approach with the inclusion of open dialogue with students in which I encouraged their questions and to share their lived experiences. I was intentional about reducing the hierarchical structures typical in classrooms by sitting with the students in a circle, being mindful of not dominating conversations, and allowing students to ask questions, reflect, and discuss.

Each student facilitated a class session during the semester using whatever materials and resources they chose to include to connect with a reading assigned from *Borderlands* and the theme for the week. I structured the course so that each student wrote a critical reading blog post entry every Tuesday and a critical reflection about the class discussions, readings, films, art, guest speakers every Thursday (see a section of the syllabus in Appendix B). All assignments were shared with each other in class, with the exception of the reflective blogs, although I did refer to them maintaining anonymity in class discussions. One of the student facilitators, for example, passed out Post-its in the circle of peers for everyone to write down one question to consider about the week's readings/discussions. We then passed and exchanged the Post-its with another student so that we all had different questions, not the ones we authored. These questions, in turn, were used to facilitate discussion for the class period. I share some of the questions here from September 25, 2018:

1. If you are considered white passing and have been treated differently, what can you do to use your privilege to support your marginalized community?

2. As a Latina minority, I feel that silence is expected. How does that affect the development of society, and what can be done to break that?

3. Is it my responsibility to help white people understand my experience?

4. How do you think other people's perceptions of you affect your personal identity in regards to race/ethnicity/gender?

5. How has identity as a woman of color affected life at Penn State? Is it different than back home?

Analysis approach: Critical self-reflection, transformation, and healing

My analysis of the data used a four-step teacher-inquiry process of description, sense-making, interpretation, and implication drawing (Dana & Yendol-Hoppey, 2014). At the end of the 16-week course, I inquired about the data collected by asking: "What did I notice about the data? What is emerging? Are there any themes that keep coming up through the data? I read through all student blog entries repeatedly and my own notes. Organically, I began to notice ideas or concepts rise to the surface: things unknown, pain, trauma, violence, frustration, vulnerability, awakening, storytelling, disempowerment, exhaustion, identities, reclaiming of self (in need of, not knowing how, or coming to terms of), expansion of perspectives and interconnectedness. Using these keywords that emerged from the data as labels for coding and sorting, I began to try and make sense of the data. This was not necessarily a clear path on how to do this—I had keywords and ideas, feelings that I was describing about the data, but what did it all mean? In what ways is this related to autohistoria-teoría and conocimiento, if at all? In the next chapter, I discuss my analysis of the *Latina Feminisms* curriculum and reflect using my own observation notes, student weekly blog reflections, anonymous student evaluations of the course and instructor.

My autohistoria-teoría: Self-theorizing in the making

The conocimiento process is an initiator for conscious work and building one's autohistoria (Anzaldúa, 2015; Zaytoun, 2015). As I have been curating my autohistoria-teoría memoir, it became necessary to develop my own framework for myself, heavily drawing on this research, my lived experiences, ancestral roots, culture, spirituality, identities and imagination. As I have critically reflected on Anzaldúa's theory of conocimiento, I understand her perspective on the fragmented self, Coyolxauhqui imperative, and the need for a process of wholeness. However, I disagree with the idea that we are fragmented individuals seeking wholeness—rather, I see my position more firmly reflected in the Taíno belief that we are born, created whole.[4] In essence,

---

[4] Taíno Indigenous people: The Taíno civilization indigenous to the Greater Antilles-Caribbean Sea (Hispaniola) flourished in the islands including Cuba, Hispaniola (Haiti and the Dominican Republic), Jamaica and Puerto Rico before and during the time when Christopher Columbus landed on the beaches of the New World in 1492. The Taíno people were targeted for genocide by the Spanish and many were killed. Many historians accredit a mass genocide and death of the Taíno ancestry, culture and beliefs at the hands of Columbus and the Spanish, however, in the last decade historians have begun to revisit this theory and realizing that the Taíno people are not only alive and active in their

our search is not for wholeness but in recognizing our whole selves. Yes, we experience pain, hurt, wounds, but as we remember over and over again that we are enough, made whole, born whole, created whole, then I can own my wholeness and be empowered through it. Wholeness as a position of who we are is an important differentiation from fragmentation—because it does not victimize; rather, it is a rising of wisdom and self-empowerment and transformation that sits at wholeness's core.

In the same way that Ata Bey, the Taíno matriarch from which all life proceeds, is whole, so are her creations. Taíno spirituality emphasizes life and experiences as interconnectedness to the past, present, and future with a vision of becoming whole and balanced in who we already are—who we were created to be. The search of our Whole Essence is a striving that Elder Ni Bon Te Ban explains, "to take back the Power of Our Lives into our Yukayekes" (Saguê-Machiran, 2016; "Introduction: Caney Circle," n.d.).

To explain the conceptual framework that I have named, Nicoari (sounds like 'Nee Koah Ree'), which means valiant, bravely spirited in Taíno vocabulary, I return to the metaphor of the Banyan tree. The Banyan tree is a taproot, meaning that it has one large deep central root system that all roots branch out from underneath, creating a network. In the same spirit in which Anzaldúa reclaims parts of her history, autohistoria, by digging through her ancestral roots, I too have been mining through history to unearth parts of my identity that have been previously unknown to me.

In my initial field research work in 2012, I went to my maternal island of Cuba to trace my Lebanese ancestors (Sotomayor, 2016). Today, my research has led me to my paternal grandmother from Puerto Rico. As I overturned stones in my research, some pieces rang familiar on my journey; the Taíno myths, proverbs, and songs that I have grown up listening to in my family, for example. Only in recent years have I heard my father, on two, maybe three, occasions admit that his mother *may* have been Taíno. Growing up, what was emphasized was my grandfather's white Spanish blood. As I examined family photos of my late abuela, I was convinced that she was or had a Taíno lineage, with her dark black, long hair, her small stature and bronze skin.

---

disbursed communities but a relevant and strong presence in indigenous culture and society in the Caribbean ("History," 2021).

I remember my abuela making my favorite dish, guanimes....

The Banyan tree is also more commonly known in the Caribbean through its Taíno name, the ceiba tree. In Boríken,[5] the name that the Taínos originally gave Puerto Rico, the ceiba, is the national tree, holding many symbolic meanings for the island with sacred Taíno beliefs. The Taíno indigenous people of Boríken believe that the ceiba tree is the balance of the world stretching its trunk through the underworld, the sea, through the earth, up into the heavens. The ceiba tree also references the Ba Coa; the wooden pole Taínos use to make holes in the ground to plant seeds for harvest. The ceiba tree is also a symbol for the Taínos' all-powerful cemi Ata Bey, Mother Earth where all life begins, a symbol of resilience, hope, love, and a ladder between worlds; a portal to ascend to a higher spiritual dimension (Rouse, 1992).

I remember as a teenager being told I was Boricua. I was confused, I did not know what that term meant. "Tu eres Boricua."? Que es eso? Boricua, "Puertorriqueña." (You are Boricua. What is that? Puerto Rican)

In 2017, Puerto Rico suffered a horrible hurricane, named Maria by meteorologists, that devastated much of the island, including Vieques, part of Puerto Rico's 51-acre coastal park where endangered mandates, sea turtles, and pelicans live and, also, was formerly a military base for the United States.[6] On Vieques, there is a 400-year-old ceiba tree regarded as the sacred history of Taíno religion. When Hurricane Maria hit in 2017, the area where the ceiba tree stood was severely devastated, left leafless and damaged, with knobby limbs broken left lying around its thick trunk. However, miraculously in early 2019, the ceiba tree bloomed its pink, lily-like blossoms offering renewed hope to Boricuas (Puerto Ricans) on the island. Ceiba trees don't bloom consistently; they need the exact conditions after the tree absorbs and stores enough energy to produce bright, sugary blossoms. La ceiba tree from Puerto Rico intensifies for me the initial metaphor of the Banyan tree. Because of the symbolism of strength, it represents a reverence towards Taíno beliefs also emerges organically through the blooming of the ceiba. I correlate the ceiba tree's conditions and nutritional needs to bloom to the educational environment that

---

[5] Boríken: the original name given by the Taíno people to what is today known as the island of Puerto Rico.

[6] Vieques, Puerto Rico: Isla de Vieques is an island of Puerto Rico, and its name is Taíno for small island. Today the island is a national wildlife refuge, but until 2003 it was internationally known as a series site for protests against the United States Navy's use of the island as a bombing range and testing ground (Ayala, 2001).

learners need to grow. Learners need all the strength and nutrients necessary to absorb in order to be able to blossom despite having endured pain, devastation, violence, and trauma. According to Taíno belief, difficulties in life, such as necessary pain allowed by Guakar, teach us strength and wisdom.[7] Taíno beliefs encompass the concept that all of life is cyclical and that we must go into ourselves to be able to go out into the world.

> *"It is through the eyes of the multiple consciousnesses of ONE that the consciousness of ALL sees ALL!" (Taíno proverb).*

One of the assignments in which learners participated in the *Latina Feminisms* class was writing and sharing their testimonios. One student shared how she grew up with the story that her Native American great-grandmother married a white man (her great-grandfather) and built a life together. However, as she researched her ancestral Native American roots, which consequently exposed that her Native American great-grandmother had been more likely kidnapped and raped at a young age by white men, it triggered something inside of her. She connected to her great-grandmother's lineage of violence and the birth of her family's generation to her own trauma and experience of being raped her first year in college, the intergenerational wound that spiritually connected the two.

It was hard to keep the tears back as I listened, reminding me of my own indigenous abuela. I remember my abuela well, making café con leche for me when I'd visit her every summer in Puerto Rico. My grandparent's home always felt lively, bright, full of laughter, and beautiful to me. I have fond memories of playing with my cousins in the front yard, going shopping to the local stores with my tias, and always expecting to see my abuelo rocking in his rocking chair on the front gated porch. I listened as my student shared with us her testimony about her great-grandmother being raped and it being normalized within her family's history for generations.

> *I suddenly remembered family stories about my abuela.*

My abuela was said to be married at 13 years old when my grandfather, a Puerto Rican with Spanish blood 14 years her senior, met her on her family's land in Utuado, Puerto Rico. He *took her as his wife*. Subsequently, they lived in

---

[7] Guakar is a warrior, the Lord of teaching trials, the spirit of tough life experiences from which we learn and mature, leading to wisdom (Rouse, 1992).

Adjuntas, a neighboring town, and she would birth fourteen children, the first one dying at a few weeks old. All of a sudden, in hearing my student's testimonio, I had the impossible thought:

> ***What if my grandmother had also been taken and raped?***
> ***What does a girl of thirteen know?***

Upon further excavation, I learned that my abuela was from Utuado, Puerto Rico, the mountainous countryside of the island rich with Taíno indigenous artifacts, beliefs, traditions, and spirituality. Ata Bey is the female creatress ancestral spirit of the Taíno people. The divine mother Ata Bey holds multiple representations of her characteristics. According to the Caney Indigenous Spiritual Circle ("Introduction: Caney Circle," n.d.), Ata Bey is the embodiment of Guar Ban Sesh (Spirit of violent Mother Nature), Ata Bey/Atabeira (mother earth, birth, fertility), Caguana (Spirit of love and affection), Karaya (Moon Spirit, human connection to the divine), and her twin sons, Yoka Hu (the Lord of life force) and Guakar (The Lord of Trials, experience, and Wisdom).

As my research continued, I asked family members questions, read about Utuado and figured out dates. I came to understand that Utuado is a prime location where Taíno culture thrived, having a strong footprint of cave drawings, cemis, and many more landscape and physical artifacts. I began learning about Taíno culture, and much of it resonated with me. I began to notice themes of Taíno spiritual beliefs, myths, and stories in my observations, reflections, and data collection. Through this student's testimonio, she chose to expose and share her wounds, her vulnerability with us. In exchange, empathy and intimacy arose within our circle for the student as she expressed her pain, knowing a part of her history stemmed from violence and trauma.

Furthermore, I was transformed as the facilitator, as I learned and came to consciousness with my abuela's memory. In heeding a call in my own consciousness, I wandered to a labyrinth in the woods near my home. In this meditative place, I began to recognize the tree in the middle of the labyrinth as the ceiba, Ata Bey. With each curve I walked in the spiral circle, the closer I became to the tree, snaking near the core, reminding me of Ata Bey.

> ***Snake, belly to the earth, Mother Earth. Shedding my skin as I go.***
> ***From the snake's mouth we are born deep from the center of her belly.***

In the labyrinth, the only way to get out is the same way you came in, reminding me of the Taíno creation story. In one part of the story, Guaguiona (the true cacique), after wandering, meets a Boitio,[8] Guabonito, who lives near a river.[9] Guaguiona must travel to the sacred chamber, Guanara[10] of Guabonito. Guaguiona is given by Guabonito; the Guanin[11] now journeys to the depths of the world of death in order to reclaim his identity. When Guabanito exchanges energies with the boitio in the depths of the world of death, they are able to be healed. Once healed, they are reborn and, while being birthed, leaving the underworld, given a new name. As they ascend from the underworld, they have initiated a profound spiritual process into an expansive consciousness allowing them passage to the three realms: upper world, middle world, and the underworld.

---

[8] Boitio is someone who is not mesmerized by the distractions of the world, and sees beyond into the World of Mystery and all things hidden. They can walk among the world and with the ancestors simultaneously ("Introduction: Caney Circle," n.d.).

[9] The River is symbolic of the Energy of Kaguana, who is love, fertility, abundance and thriving-the embodiment of Feminine Energy.

[10] Guanara is the sacred cave of the Mother Earth.

[11] Guanin: symbolic of the bright and shining sun and symbol of Cacique.

Chapter 5

Decolonial feminist teaching in seven acts

I curated the curriculum with Anzaldúa's seven transformative acts of conocimiento in conjunction with *Borderlands* (1999); I also included sub-themes pulled from the book that were relevant as supporting materials and resources such as popular culture, identity, race, sexuality, art, violence, labor, borders, migration, and visual culture. I delineate in this section the recursive transformative acts of conocimiento in conjunction with the syllabus (see Appendix C, the *Latina Feminisms* Syllabus and Appendix D, the Assignment Descriptions). Anzaldúa writes about a silence that needs to be transformed—but before that can happen, it needs to travel our (female) bodies for the transformation to occur. In *Making Face, Making Soul* (1990), Anzaldúa writes:

> For silence to be transformed into speech, sounds, and words, it must first traverse through our female bodies. For the body to give birth to utterance, the human entity must recognize itself as carnal—skin, muscles, entrails, brain, belly. Because our bodies have been stolen, brutalized or numbed, it is difficult to speak from/through them. (Anzaldúa, 1990, p. xxii)

I liken the themes, materials, and topics in the *Latina Feminisms* course to the 'silence' which Anzaldúa writes about as a way to: (a) expose learners to the lineage of silencing historically, and (b) to facilitate a threshold crossing destabilizing perceived realities. I interpret my facilitating of exposing silences as initiating the first transformative acts of the conocimiento process, susto/fear, arrebato (fury, rapture, gust). Because the academic canons in education marginalize underrepresented voices and colonialism has 'brutalized' our bodies, the silence must first be digested. Students needed to process, self-reflect, and absorb the enormity of such historical contexts as to allow it to 'traverse' through their bodies. The following are my analyses of my curriculum and decolonial feminist teaching organized by the seven acts of my curating, beginning with arrebato susto.

Curating transformative act one: Arrebato susto

The assignments I curated for the course are designed for students to critically self-reflect about internal and external bursts of fury that emerge from the silences that are exposed and brought out of the shadows. Through learners' reflective writing, poetry, testimonios, and class discussions, the digestion of silence is facilitated. Because of the trauma that colonialism and racism (discrimination) impart on disenfranchised bodies, it is "difficult to speak from/through them" (Anzaldúa, 1990, p. xix). But it is in the speech, the words, the "sending of our voices, visuals, and visions outward into the world, we alter the walls and make them a framework for new windows and doors" (Anzaldúa, 1990, p. xxv). Only then, after the silences are voiced, felt, and realized, can a birth to utterance come to be.

The class discussed the historical contexts for labels in the U.S., new trends in changing or evolving labels such as Latina/o and Chicanoism, and the significance and implications of imposed labels versus self-identifying labels and autonomy. Three out of the ten students identifying as Latina/o/x or Hispanic shared their personal insights and family position on the topic of identity labels in relation to generational significance. Furthermore, understanding the power dynamics between over and under-privileged groups was necessary for uncovering the depth of past and current contexts through a political, national, and global lens. Learners and curators/educators engaged in course materials, which invited a critical self-reflection and challenged colonizing bias history, must recognize and accept a new or different reality. It is difficult to accept a different reality when all that has been absorbed and consumed before a given point was so vastly different, shaped by systemic discriminating powers. The simple fact that U.S. history taught in many institutions in the U.S. excludes voices and identities of non-White, heterosexual, male bodies and histories which challenge and resist different realities is proof of the inequity and disenfranchisement of power; a willed ignorance, desconocimientos.

Curating transformative act two: Nepantla

Learning about Latin America and the Caribbean's historical timeline and its violent relationship to the U.S., we were catapulted into nepantla; the second transformative act is when new realities emerged, and doubts and questions continued to surface. In discussing Nicaragua, Cuba, Chile, Dominican Republic, and Mexico's revolutions, dictatorships, struggle for autonomy, and U.S. interventions juxtaposed to Jose Martí's[1] vision for a unified Latin America and

---

[1] Jose Martí was a Cuban poet, essayist, journalist, translator, professor and publisher who is considered a national hero and important Latin American national hero and his literature. He is considered an important revolutionary philosopher and political theorist. Martí advocated for Cuba's bid for independence against Spain, he died in Cuba, in battle for independence in 1895. He traveled extensively to Spain, Latin America and the United

Caribbean, the stark reality became entangled with trauma and violence. We watched *Las Madres de Plaza de Mayo*, a documentary that explains the disappearance of over 30,000 young students and Argentinean citizens during the Dirty War in Argentina (Navarro, 1989; D'Alessandro, 1998; Bosco, 2006).[2] The connection between the documentary of *Las Madres* and Anzaldúa's theories of the wound, Borderlands and transformative acts is in recognizing trauma and pain in various ways. *Las Madres* is about spiritual activism, breaking the silence, resisting, finding a voice in collaboration with others and self, building community, among many other layers of oppression and liberations. Anzaldúa's Borderland theory discusses entanglements with race, and the concept of homeland, both geographical and imagined, as *Borderlands* (1999), chapter one situates Aztlán[3] and the border as an open wound. Anzaldúa's Borderland theory transcends physical, emotional, psychological, and spiritual borders. I also included nostalgic memories within Borderland Theory because I situated the open wound as often a place of trauma and retracing oneself to other entities that may be passed down generationally through nostalgia and/or memory crossings. As in my own experiences with my Lebanese ancestry or deep connection with my Cuban roots from my mother and maternal relatives, despite not going to Cuba until much later in my adult life.

My students experienced the concept of the open wound when watching the compilation of art performances in *The Couple in the Cage* (1992) by Coco Fusco and Guillermo Gómez-Peña, a satirical commentary on cultural stereotyping and colonizing production of culture and the savage. In the performances, Fusco and Gómez-Peña toured five countries as they were

---

States, living for long periods in Spain and the U.S. as well as Cuba (Martí-Parreño, Méndez-Ibáñez, & Alonso-Arroyo, 2016; Martí, 2002; Font & Quiroz, 2006).

[2] The Mothers of the Plaza de Mayo/Asociación Madres de Plaza de Mayo is an association of Argentine mothers whose children "disappeared" during the state terrorism of the military dictatorship between 1976-1983. The mothers' group was founded by Azucena Villaflor with support from French nuns Alicia Doyon and Léonie Duquet, subsequently they were kidnapped, tortured, and murdered by the Argentine military government. The mothers organized while trying to learn what had happened to their children and began to march in 1977 at the Plaza de Mayo in Buenos Aires in front of the presidential palace in a public defiance of the governments state terrorism intended to silence all in opposition. Wearing white head scarves to symbolize the diaper of their lost children, the mothers marched in solidarity to protest the atrocities committed by the military government. The Mothers of the Plaza de Mayo was the first major group to organize against human rights violations impacting women's role in protesting for human, political and civil rights violations on a global scale throughout Latin America (Navarro, 1989; D'Alessandro, 1998; Bosco, 2006).

[3] Atzlán, The Plan Espiritual de Aztlán is a pro-indigenist manifesto advocating Chicano nationalism and self-determination for Mexican Americans.

locked in a cage in 'primitive' costumes acting as two undiscovered Amerindians (Taylor, 1998). Throughout the compilation of performances, the audience was interviewed to comment on what they observed in the many museums and public spaces exhibited. The audience members were not told that the exhibit was an art performance. The mixture of responses documented ranged from audience members being intrigued, curious, accepting of the exhibit as legitimate, stretching to the other extreme of outrage, unbelievability, and reproduction of enslavement and colonization. The students were not told that the film was a satirical performance. By the end, most students understood the premise of the performance as it was exposed in the film. The students' reactions were visible as they felt indignation and how preposterous audience members reacted by joining in and supporting the cage couple as primitive, savage specimens. The students also expressed how some interviewed audience members were clearly triggered by past cultural trauma and violence towards Native Americans and African slave histories in the U.S. and Europe.

As a class, we discussed the triggering of generational trauma as students shared emotional stories of violence that parents, grandparents, and family members had experienced because of migration, exile, displacement, and trans-living—a cost towards a better life for themselves and their future generations. Through the student-led narratives of pain, hurt, and the open wounds of 'crossings', I witnessed the definition of the Border as one that is expansive. Students' memories ranged from religious, political, cultural, socio-economic, and physical experiences in the U.S., Europe, Latin America, the Caribbean. The range of experiences from various socio-economic statuses, religious views, political climates, and geographical locations reminded me of human vulnerability and interconnections. I noted, "[s]tudents always surprise me as they share pieces of themselves that are raw, private, and painful" (September 20, 2018). Through stories of old memories, students retraced parts of themselves that extended back in their historical lineages, connecting borderlands to a nostalgia that, once remembered, becomes part of their awakened consciousness. Students awakened consciousness, or conocimiento through their connections of the aforementioned 'border crossings', becomes a fragment of their identity, experiences, and part of their autohistoria.

Curating transformative act three: The Coatlicue state

Identity and sexuality was the focused theme in the third transformative act of the Coatlicue state, chapter three, and part of chapter four that students read in *Borderlands* (Anzaldúa, 1999). Students wrote and shared their identity poems about any perspective of their life they chose. It became evident that the similar thread among the poems spoke about some type of pain, memory, and/or history. I included the identity poem assignment for students to critically self-reflect and assess parts of who they believe they are. One of the components of the Coatlicue state is confronting shadows and resisting, leading to multiple ways of re-envisioning ourselves (transformation). Many themes emerged from students' identity poems, such as citizenship, not-belonging, nostalgia, minority, identity, pain, bi-nationalism, sexual violence, stereotypes, memory, history, bloodlines, colonization, imperialism, and privilege (September 20, 2019). The themes that came through the student poems were unpacked through student facilitation in conjunction with the Coatlicue state, la facultad, and spirituality. Curiosity among the students arose about physical implications on the body being connected with oppressions, pain, and trauma, a type of syncretism that exists between the mind, body, soul, and spirit.

I invited the LGBTQA+ guest speakers, the Student Voice panel to our class, where three students shared their entangled testimonios around sexual identities, coming out, and resistance/acceptance. The undergraduate student guests shared vulnerable sides of themselves through narratives of critically self-reflecting about their sexual orientations, challenges and resistance they encountered in their life thus far, and the impact on their daily lived experiences. The panel introduced a broad overview of the various ways sexual orientation may be labeled and experienced on a wide spectrum. The value I find in students actively listening to each other testimonios is profound. The questions and conversations that arose from these shared stories added another layer of realizing new perspectives and empathy.

We screened the film and read *Brincando el charco* (1999) by Frances Negron-Muntaner, "When I Was a Puerto Rican Lesbian. Meditations on *Brincando el Charco.*" In this film, many class themes were intertwined; for example, Gay rights movement in Puerto Rico is contextualized, religious traditions within a Puerto Rican family, machismo, the in-betweenness of the U.S. mainland, and colonized Puerto Rican territory. Implications about citizenship, language code-switching, and sexual identities were all conversations unpacked in class discussions and students' critical reflections. Parallels were made to *Borderlands* (Anzaldúa. 1999) as Anzaldúa, and Negron-Muntaner code switched in their work between English and dialects of Spanish. Negron-Muntaner's film *Brincando el Charco* (1999) offered a visual example of living in the gap, the in-betweenness of cultures, country, language, displacement, sexual identity, and lived experiences. Negron-Muntaner's film exposes multiple layers of a Puerto Rican Lesbian's lived experiences between her expulsion from her family by her father's patriarchal homophobic home in Puerto Rico and her new life on the mainland (United States) as a Puerto Rican Lesbian photographer. *Brincando el Charco* (1999) juxtaposed with Anzaldúa's writing of Coatlalopeuh, the central deity connected to Indian ancestry and descendent of the earth goddesses, Coatlicue. Discussing Negron-Muntaner's and Anzaldúa's work together creates an interesting analysis of the violent patriarchal Azteca-Mexica culture. Azteca refers to the people who came from Aztlan, the origin of the Aztec people, while Mexica refers to pre-Colombian Mexico. Using the term Azteca-Mexica is challenging and resisting a normative narrative that does not value these indigenous cultures. Similar to using the Taíno names of Boríken and Boricua[4] as a form of resistance and acknowledgment of indigenous roots (like the Banyan tree) that are still observed and living. In the Azteca-Mexica culture, strong, powerful female deities were demonized and exiled to underground worlds and substituted with male deities (Anzaldúa, 1999). Because of the displacement of female deities, Anzaldúa explains that the female Self and the female deities were split, causing a disconnect. Perhaps, my students wondered, the disconnect between Self and deities is what we experience as a disconnect between our spirit, mind, soul, and body because of historical trauma and wounds.

Curating transformative act four: Reframing

I curated the fourth transformative act, a call to action, by inviting local Mexican-American artist Bessie Floresgomez into our class to share her local research, documentary short films, and photography. Floresgomez interviewed and documented seasonal farm workers from Central and South America, some of which work the farms in the Centre Hall, Pennsylvania area. She shared her experience gathering stories from seasonal farm workers in Mexico and Pennsylvania, their journeys north, and their realities in their home countries. My decision to invite Floresgomez was to highlight what Anzaldúa writes of "invoking art" or a shamanic practice of art as intertwined within everyday life (Anzaldúa, 1999, p. 88). A twofold decision, Floresgomez engaged, first in a discussion about components of seasonal farm workers in the local area and the complexities of their lived realities and feelings of in-betweenness. Secondly, her short documentary films and photographs were powerful fragments of narratives breaking the silences and stereotypes around Brown bodies from South and Central America as violent, othered, and lazy. For example, photographs of maimed bodies connected to discussions of violence, the dangers of crossing the U.S./Mexico border, and the perseverance for a better life at often high costs. Organically, Floresgomez, at the prompting by student questions, shared with us her own experiences as a Mexican migrating to the North and her struggles as she has grappled with identity, family heritage, citizenship, and assimilation.

---

[4] Boricua is the Taíno word for those from Boríken, or Puerto Rico.

In the *Borderlands* chapters, "How to tame a wild tongue" and "Overcoming the tradition of silence," the old tools of oppression are challenged and broken by awareness of the oppressions and the trauma-induced onto oneself and then the reorganizing of lived experiences to create meaning for oneself (Anzaldúa, 1999, pp. 75-77). For example, one student shared her struggles to speak up for herself, something she had been encouraged not to do. However, after critically self-reflecting, she realized that her 'wild tongue' is a part of who she is and valuing self and respecting self is critical for her self-empowering (see Figure 5.1). I interpret the confrontation of her shadows and recognize the strength that had been buried as a call to action to herself and to reach out to others. She shared on her critical reflection blog:

> As someone who has only ever known how to speak one language, I don't necessarily identify with her struggles. But that doesn't mean I don't identify with the idea of finding your sense of self through speech and language. I've always been a talker, and as a result, a strong part of my identity is my voice. In order for me to respect myself as a human, I have to respect my wild tongue. After 20 years of being told I need to think before I speak, I am learning that my voice and my intuition are a powerful tool I can use to help others and learn more about myself (R.C. September 11, 2018).

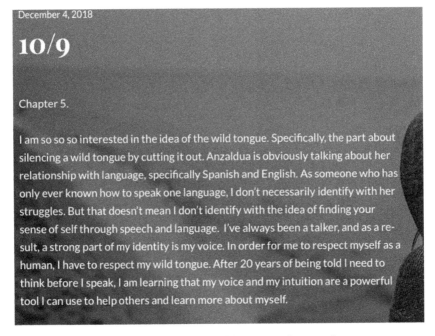

Figure 5.1. Critical reflection blog excerpt from student.

One of the biggest take-aways that I journaled about after Bessie's visit was her explanation of how she never really thought about her identity as Mexican until she came to the United States. In the U.S., she feels a strong conviction not to let her seeds (children) fall in the branches but rather have a strong connection to their roots.

Curating transformative act five: Autohistoria-teoria

Autohistoria is the telling of ourselves, our testimonios, the fifth transformative act, is creating a new story for ourselves out of the fragments and valuing of Self. Anzaldúa explains that writing for herself makes meaning of her traumas, allowing her to re-imagine in new ways, and allowing for transformation to be in effect (Anzaldúa, 1999). She explains, "I write the myths in me, the myths I am, the myths I want to evoke" and claims that the combination of the words, the images, and the feelings all have an energy and power in reshaping our realities (Anzaldúa, 1999, p. 93). Writing, Anzaldúa claims, is a constant transformative cycle of making meaning out of our experiences into a "numinous experience" where another path is opened (Anzaldúa, 1999, p. 95).

I encouraged the analysis of what Anzaldúa terms a shamanic state and a sensuous act through writing and correlated this concept to what we had been doing; critically reflecting, reading, and looking inwardly at our consciousness. In order to envision new possibilities and autohistorias, the past needs to be recursively re-evaluated, confronted, and digested for new perspectives on the spiral are to be made known. Just as perspectives change depending on where one is in life, as if walking in a labyrinth, so may we envision new stories. In the journey of the fifth transformative act, autohistoria, students wrote and shared their testimonios, a defining moment in their lives where something happened that changed or impacted their life. For example, one student shared his experience of coming out to his close friends as bisexual but had not done so with his family because of fear of their traditional view of sexuality. By the end of the semester, when he presented his creative poster project, he shared how he planned to talk with his family and share a part of his identity that he had feared for so long (see Figure 5.2).

During the last week of classes, each student presented their creative poster (see Figure 5.3), which they designed about a theme(s) that we discussed or touched on during the semester in connection with Anzaldúa's (1999) *Borderlands* and an aspect of their lived experience. My curatorial decision to assign a creative poster (see Figure 5.4) as a final individual project germinated from a few thought seeds. I envisioned a way that could be a visual representation of a transformative conocimiento theory as a metaphor for autohistoria-teoría, a re-organizing of an individual's fragments of lived experiences with autonomy, theorizing, and agency. The creative poster is making sense of a component(s) of an aspect of one's life with purpose and inspiration towards transformation, the theorizing of their lived experiences. Each student decided whether they wanted to create a digital or physical poster and needed to present it to the class circle explaining their concept, symbols, and theorizing of their creative interpretation of an aspect of their life. It was here, in the last weeks of class and wrapping up the semester with the final creative project, that I was able to realize some of the blooms, or at least germination of seeds, within the students. The final presentations exceeded my expectations, excitedly awaited students' reflections and their sharing of their experiences. In the future, I would open the format up more so that it wouldn't have to be a poster but any creative representation that they would be inspired to.

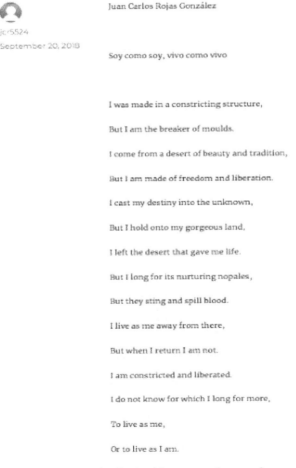

Figure 5.2. Critical reflection blog excerpt from student.

Figure 5.3. Critical reflection blog excerpt from student.

Figure 5.4. Creative Poster by student.

Curating transformative act six: Renewing

Curating a new story to the world and testing it marks the sixth transformative act of conocimiento. I curated this transformative act with the sub-themes of tracing ancestral roots and lived experiences on the border and in-between and complex notions of citizenship, identities, and the multiplicitous self. Like the Banyan tree root metaphor and the complexities of germination, host, and colonizing tree, border crossing, as Anzaldúa reminds us, is a struggle. Students discussed Ruth Behar's (2002) documentary, Adio Kerida/Goodbye Dear Love, through critical reflection blog entries as Behar engages in border crossings between her Cuban, Jewish, and American roots (see Figure 5.5). Behar's journey of remembering self through heritage and cultural identity migrating to the United States from Cuba at a young age is about crossing back and forth throughout her life, physically, emotionally, psychologically, and through memory and nostalgia.

Figure 5.5. Cover of Ruth Behar's documentary, Adio Kerida.

Our class discussions were contextualized by sharing my own research and experiences in Cuba, which originated with my own search for my ancestral Lebanese roots in 2011. Allowing for analysis of complexities within the Cuban government, policies with the U.S., and the economic landscape of Cuba, broadly defined, we, as a class, were able to dive into discussions of globalization and transnationalism deeply. In sharing my own lived experiences and knowledge about Cuba, students were able to witness how I am practicing autohistoria-teoría**Error! Bookmark not defined.**. Through listening to varied testimonios throughout the semester, including Behar and my own, students situated these experiences as often painful, as another student wrote: "[Ruth Behar] [a]ims to lift an "emotional embargo" that has kept Cubans silent, through the medium of storytelling as well as poetry and art" (October 16, 2018). Students recognized the entanglements of oppression due to border crossing, as one student, in reflecting on Behar's work, wrote:

> Ruth Behar's *Adio Kerida,* she talks about her Jewish grandparents migrating from Europe to Cuba in the 1920s to escape antisemitism, and being permitted in Cuba only because white Cuban leaders feared the dark skinned AfroCubans becoming too powerful. Her entire Cuban ancestry – painful as it is on its own – can only exist because of systematic racism. (P.R. October 16, 2018)

I expanded the contexts of the border crossing between the United States and Latin American countries and the Caribbean with readings that account for different types of violence outside of the United States but are laced with U.S.A politics and economy. These aided discussions about impact, responsibilities, and accountability between border crossings, embodiment, and the spiritual. Connections between violence and labor on borders emerged as a prominent theme, as a student wrote:

> [W]omen, regardless of the amount of agency they had, were forced to bare the pain of the economy on their bodies. Factories and chemicals, violence, and the environment take a toll on health and the spirit (R.C. October 23, 2018).

The interconnectedness that students were able to discern from the testimonios shared, read, and heard in class emerged from conscious work of critically reflecting and dialogue.

In curating the syllabus, I wanted to make sure that violence was defined in a myriad of ways. This is important because, as a society and culture, we have become desensitized to what violence may mean. I invited a guest speaker, Jennifer Pencek, from the Gender Equity Center, who facilitated a class discussion on defining violence in various contexts and scenarios, gender inequality, and resources on our campus to support students. This proved to be so relevant and significant for our class that students afterward inquired why they (a) never knew about the center and their work, (b) why was the information that Pencek shared about our university was not mandatory information upon entering campus, and (c) the definitions for various scenarios of what constitutes sexual violence, harassment, and assault were new to most students. Students shared (predominantly the female identity students and LGBTQ+ identifying students) how they had been at some point in their lives a victim of sexual violence. One student shared about a moment in his life where he had to transfer college campuses because a person became infatuated with him and was stalking and disrupting his life. He became vulnerable in sharing such experiences that resist and challenge heteronormative narratives and open dialogue to the various types of violence and abuse. Another White male student (identifying as heterosexual) was quite shocked at the information, students' experiences and verbally shared in class the following:

> [he] I had no idea that many of these things explained constituted a type of violence—they are so normalized in many ways—and I [he] am shocked that these are what seem to be common experiences by most of us in this room. (R. D., October 29, 2018)

Another student expressed in her reflective blog how she recently had an experience of hearing a woman scream while being raped across the river to where she lives. The student's response was to call the police immediately. She wrote, "[t]he ruptures over that event, over talking to the [police] about what I heard, is too prevalent in my mind to consider crossing the river" (L.L., October 30, 2018). The trauma, to the victim and the witness, was for my student paralleled to the concept of crossing—crossing the river, crossing trauma, crossing pain, crossing violence.

Curating transformative act seven: Nepantlera

The transformative struggle embodied in various ways throughout the conocimiento stages is enacted again in the seventh transformative act in becoming a crosser. As a class, we visited the Palmer Museum of Art on our Penn State campus to view and discuss an art exhibit I curated for our *Latina Feminisms* course. Upon meeting in the museum lobby, students were paired off and given a strip of paper that had one of the seven transformative acts of the conocimiento theory written on it. The pairs of students were encouraged to walk the two-story museum and find a work of art that they felt represented their given transformation act and theorize to the class how or why they believe this. We met again twenty minutes later, walking together to each piece of artwork chosen as the pairs of students explained their rationale.

I chose to include, *Dreaming in Cuban* (1992) by Christina García towards the end of the semester because the novel ties together many perspectives discussed throughout the semester. Through various voices: on the Cuban government, North American assimilation, and the crossings back and forth between memory, longing, and survival as the novel is a constant transformative struggle of becoming and creating meaning in the characters' complex Cuban and Cuban-American identities. We discussed the novel *Dreaming in Cuban*

(1992*)* as layered with many themes, such as intergenerational family relationships between Cuba and the United States, the concepts of susto and la facultad, magical realism, historical Cuban contexts, testimonios, nostalgia, domestic violence, memory, heritage, culture, spirituality, migration, loss, and the process of healing. Students connected this novel to their own lived experiences. One student reflected on the domestic violence and abuse issues throughout the book, the roles that victims and abusers play and the impact on their children. She wrote:

> For me, this is reminiscent of my childhood, and likely the childhood of other children who are abused by one or both parents or whose parents have had an immature, unsettled divorce. When I was a child, my father would hit me and throw me down the stairs, much like he had done to my mother before she left him, but he also spoke to me as if my mother was the "bad parent." He convinced me at one point that she didn't love me and that I should live with him, even though objectively, he was hurting and abusing me. As an observer to *Dreaming in Cuban,* it is very hard to figure out which parent is good or bad, or if that dichotomy even exists (F.K., November 15, 2019).

I interpret this critical reflection blog post as signifying a tension between experiences and normalized binaries that we (as a society) have socially constructed. This blog post also made me aware of the many triggers that may exist within classroom materials and how a student engages with the materials can be a vulnerable and fragile site.

The previously mentioned student was triggered when reading the novel *Dreaming in Cuban* and was met with a flashback of abuse in her childhood. Furthermore, the trigger that the student experienced caused them to question the binary of good/bad, which allegedly created the painful memory. The doubting of the binary and revisiting of their traumatic abusive past is what Anzaldúa writes in her conocimiento theory, where all the parts of oneself become unstable, shifting, and you cannot go back to the way things were once you awake consciously. This student's entry also suggests that in reexamining the fragments of their life, the narrative that had been playing is not interrupted, revealing itself to be more complicated and different from what was perceived before, in doing so, the story is changed, and they (the student) has the autonomy to reframe their experience as they cross back and forth, as a mediator in their own life of what was and what could be.

Chapter 6

Transformative learning
and curatorial pillars

In this chapter, I reflect on my decolonial feminist teaching. I organized this chapter according to the tenants of transformative learning that I define as curatorial pillars of a *Latina Feminism* course, which are: a call for awakening, vulnerability to self and others, wandering/sense of not-belonging, healing, and interconnectedness. I analyzed the process towards transformative learning by studying students' critical reflection blog entries, looking carefully for clues that may suggest new ways of thinking, perceiving, or understanding self, other, education, society, or culture. I was also reading for ways students find connections (the interconnectedness) between their own lived experiences and others' experiences in a way that may find collective or connected paths.

My conceptual framework for both the curriculum and my teaching, birthed from my autohistoria-teoría**Error! Bookmark not defined.** testimonio and Anzaldúa's theories of autohistoria and conocimiento, formed the parameters in which I structured my syllabus. In curating a *Latina Feminisms* syllabus, I had certain points in mind that I wanted to be sure to address in a class that had not been taught at the Pennsylvania State University for more than eight years. I was also mindful of my physical embodiment in the classroom as a Latina and Feminist, as I do not attempt to conceal some of my identities, such as ethnicity and standpoint. For many students who have experienced similarities to my own, I was the first Latina they have met who is pursuing a graduate school, pursuing a doctorate degree and teaching a *Latina Feminisms* course, which is their first undergraduate course in this subject area. My physical positionally in a predominantly White institution is significant because, in many ways, I am representing for many a historical context that learners know very little about. By engaging learners to become aware of their own privilege and power, I hope we/students will reflect on their ignorance and separation from their own roots due to colonialism and a White supremacist education. For this reason, I am intentional about discussing the entanglements of our identities as multiple and complex—my aim, in facilitating and guiding conversations within the course is a collective journey is not one to find answers but rather to dig deep into ourselves in an effort towards empathy, transformation, and the process of healing.

A call for awakening

In reality, we all experience 'a call for awakening' in various ways throughout our life. As a curator of a course environment, one of my responsibilities is 'staging' the call for awakening through a more 'formal' approach because the course is 16 weeks with time parameters. A call for awakening is important because it is something that occurs, the whisper that is heard, the shaking that wakes one up from sleep. For the Taínos, the call for awakening is symbolic through a seashell trumpet that defies time and borders; the purpose is to awaken the sleeping consciousness or clarity for the confused. For example, one of my calls of awakening was when, at 31, I decided to go to college and take a Women's Studies introduction course, gifting me voices that understood me, and I them, for the first time.

To initiate 'a call for awakening' during the first class, I did two things to begin to set in motion the first curatorial pillar, a call for awakening—the sense that there is something else lurking beneath all you think you know. The first was sharing a part of my testimonio, situating where I am coming from through my own lived experiences, and what it means for me to curate the syllabus and curriculum for the Latina Feminisms class. I also gave a historical overview of how the Latina Feminisms class fits into Penn State's academic history. I first took the Latina Feminisms class as an undergraduate about eight years prior to teaching it myself, under my first Latina faculty mentor. The course had not been offered for eight years because the faculty and graduate teaching assistants during that period of eight years were not scholars of Latina Feminisms to be in the position to teach the course. The Latina Feminisms class was the first classroom space to truly validate my identity and experiences in a way I never knew existed; a liberating, self-actualizing, and self-empowering experience.

I began the first week of classes with an interactive lecture titled, "No Representation *is* Representation,"[1] as I focused on social movements that have occurred in the United States post-1950s. I shared a general historical timeline of events in the United States pertaining to relations with Latin America and the Caribbean. Most students were not familiar with the majority of the U.S. movements I shared. I noticed learners taking notes fervently as they then began to ask questions such as: Who? Why? Why haven't I heard of these things in my education thus far? Who does know about them? Why do some of

---

[1] No Representation *is* Representation is the name of an interactive art lecture I gave in class whereby examining activist art post 1960s social movements, as a class, we engaged in a dialogue about the things we know and do not know, critically reflecting on why.

us know these historical events but not others? Why am I not being represented? Or why am I being represented like *that*?

In discussing the binaries that exist in our cultures and society (gender, sex, class, etc.) at the beginning of the semester, we (as a class) were able to better untangle why binaries are part of an oppressive system that does not speak accurately to many lived experiences and ignores others. Asking the questions; how do I fit into these binaries? What happens if I don't? My role is to mediate and facilitate class discussions and critical self-reflection writing through student blogs that bring to light the possibility for new perspectives about privilege, power, and identifying and unpacking oppressive systems. Through this process of critical self-reflections and dialogues, parts of our testimonios begin to reveal themselves.

Chapter seven in *Borderlands/La Frontera* (1999) is entitled, "Towards a New Consciousness" Anzaldúa posits that we first need to dismantle the binaries or there can be "no real healing of our psyches" (Anzaldúa, 1999, p. 106). My aim to disrupt the binaries in the classroom is an intentional decision to bring to light what often we (as individuals/collectives) fall outside, in-between the binaries, *not* within them. As students walk into the classroom, I ask them to please pick up a piece of chalk and write on the chalkboard any and all labels they use for themselves as identity markers. I initiate the request by writing my self-identity labels. Many learners comment on how they need to think about this for a minute because they really hadn't given it much thought. This simple activity facilitates the discussion that follows: Why do they identify the way they do? Which I follow-up with, what if you do not fall into one category? Many students, if not all, realize and reflect that they do not fall into strictly one category. This discussion initiates several topics (lived experiences, sexuality, gender, sex, racial identity, national/citizenship, class, etc.) about binaries that are unpacked, eventually defining our entangled identities (Knight, 2007) and W.E.B. Du Bois's concept of double-consciousness.[2]

Historically, through the lens of the United States, theorizing and knowledge building has been in the hands of dominant Anglo culture, and the knowledge of people of color has been systematically excluded (Hurtado, 2003). Because of historical exclusion, it is critical to create and hold theorizing spaces where, through "our own approach and methodologies, we transform that theorizing space" (Anzaldúa, 1990, p. xxv). By theorizing (making sense) of our experiences, we are re-searching ourselves, our historical contexts, and critically reflecting on

---

[2] Double Consciousness, a term introduced by W. E. B. Du Bois (repr. 2006) in [190]3, refers to the way in which you are perceived, and who you see yourself do not match: the tension that you have more than one social identity.

self and our social realities. Autohistoria-teoría is a process and path to rewriting histories and crossing borders with new knowledge and methods for theorizing. Autohistoria-teoría is a way to navigate in-between spaces and to critically look at situations and their contexts (revealing their underpinnings) in "forming our own categories and theoretical models for patterns we uncover" (Anzaldúa, 1990, p. xxv). Pitts (2016) explains the creative meaning-making process of autohistoria-teoría as entangled when she explains, "autohistoria is presented as a difficult task, and one that involves critically interrogating one's own social position within embedded frameworks of meaning- and knowledge-production" (p. 364). I extend Pitts's interpretation of autohistoria beyond embedding "frameworks of meaning" to an *embodiment* of knowledge-production and modes of meaningful frameworks. Therefore, decolonial feminist facilitators have the responsibility to model the embodiment of a decolonizing pedagogy.

Vulnerability

In my teaching, I observed that when students are aware of their history and share their experiences, they become vulnerable, and through the shared vulnerability, can develop empathy because they see the humanity in each other, disregarding any differences, which can lead to self-empowerment, healing,[3] and a sense of belonging in the world and to one's self. I guided student participation in various ways to accommodate diverse learners in the course. Writing a blog entry that only the instructor will read may feel more comfortable for some learners than actively engaging in class discussions or asking questions. Aside from the blog entries, all other assignments were shared with the class. Although understanding that some students may not feel comfortable sharing in class, I feel that it is important to have this as an integral part because it is one way in which to facilitate a sense of vulnerability, intimacy, and empathy.

Students expressed how many concepts they had never reflected on previously all of a sudden emerged for them as embodied knowing. As a curator, I witnessed students' self-reflective process and interconnectedness from an assignment such as writing and sharing testimonios. For example, after testimonios were shared by students in the class, we paused and reflected on all that was shared and heard. A collective effort of beginning to theorize our experiences, autohistoria-teoría began to take form as students began to discuss with each other about their experiences. For example, one student wrote, "[i]t was interesting to see how most of the experiences were influenced

---

[3] Healing as a process.

by some kind of social issue, whether it was domestic violence, toxic relationships, mental health, or health disparities." Students reflected and commented on how they had never had an experience in sharing their vulnerabilities in a class setting before. Anzaldúa explains, in what she refers to as the fifth stage, the process of re-writing our narratives extends beyond the self, "When creating a personal narrative, you also co-create the group/cultural story" (Anzaldúa & Keating, 2009, p. 560).

The identity poem exercise was valuable in the continued inner work of critical self-reflection and conscious awakening. In the process of students turning inward and critically reflecting on their own lived experiences and multiple identities, they began to formulate a vocabulary for themselves, making connections they had not made prior. For example, one student began to realize that her upbringing as one of the only Latinas in a predominantly Asian school growing up impacted her identity, inducing academic pressure as a student because of the rigorous competitive education. She shared how the experiences of her K-12 education shaped her identity in a myriad of ways, including her college career pursuing engineering in a top university. She admitted that although she did not like her chosen major, she was on the engineering trajectory as a child with little agency to do anything else. Furthermore, she explained her sense of not belonging in her school and felt an in-betweenness living in a predominantly Spanish-speaking Hispanic/Latina community and family, but being educated in a predominantly Asian school in the United States.

Most students expressed their apprehensions about the class shared assignments, specifically the identity poem, testimonio, and creative poster. Because my boundaries for the assignments were so broad and allowed for creative interpretation, students found this to be a non-traditional approach inquiring from me what I was looking for. I assured them repeatedly that there was no wrong way to interpret each assignment; on the contrary, each interpretation and translation of the assignment as they saw fit was valid. Although apprehension was felt at the beginning of many of these assignments, students curated their interpretations in unpredictable ways. For example, after learners shared their identity poems in class, there was silence. Then, a comment broke the silence from one of the students as she shared how much closer, connected, and vulnerable she feels in the group—a feeling she has never experienced in a class setting. Through the remaining discussions that day, as more students shared, I was reminded of Lorna Dee Cervantes's poem, "To the young white man who asked how I, an Intelligent Woman believe in the war between races" (1994). I stood up from my seat and pulled the poem up on our computer screen. I quickly found the reading of the poem on YouTube, and we listened. As a class, we then took out our writing instruments to critically self-reflect on the class and the week's discussions. In my journal reflection, I wrote:

> We cry together, we reflect on what we've heard—our differences and commonalities. Our struggles—privileges—pain. I believe this is what Anzaldúa means by healing through our wounds or at least one manifestation of it (field notes, October 18, 2018).

The complexities that occurred in the before mentioned moments in class, I interpret as straddling the creative acts through the performativity of students reading their identity poems. The act of listening to each other, sitting in silence and then as a collective body writing and hearing Lorna Dee Cervantes poem being amplified in the classroom space and read aloud by multiple voices and accompanied by various images are all expressions of creative acts coming together. The creative acts that emerged in that moment of time within the classroom space, I also interpret as transformative acts being traveled as a collective embodiment. For example, the transformative act of susto being traveled as each voice shared out loud a part of their identity. Or as a collective we traveled as a class into the individual's 'world' for a moment. Or perhaps, the transformative act of nepantla, in being in-between worlds.

A sense of belonging/wandering

Because the class size for this research was an ideal small group (10 students), the physical and psychological space felt intimate. From the first class we shared, I emphasized that what is shared during our class time is to stay within our class and not to share anyone else's stories outside of class. Students gave consent to being part of my research and dissertation and understood that their contributions would become part of research publication. Although I advocate for a safer classroom environment,[4] I am also aware of the power dynamics that may prohibit this. For example, gender and sexual identity dynamics may not allow for full integration of a safer classroom space if any of the students have experienced violence, hate, or discrimination; or if students belong to a dominant group, this may impede some students not part of the dominant group from feeling safer. I felt a sense of apprehension, particularly with one White male student who disclosed his privileged socio-economic status and

---

[4] I define safe houses/spaces in this study as "[L]ocations where people can go and not feel threatened. They are sites where people may share their experiences in the contact zone with those who have had similar experiences and can empathize" (Knight, 2007, p. 24).

carried himself with similar traits to an Alpha male.[5] As the semester progressed, this seemed to become more visible and was unpacked further through class discussions with topics of hyper-masculinity, male privilege, and machismo. My initial concern was that if any person in the class had been a victim of sexual harassment, assault, and/or violence that they may be triggered or refrain from engaging in class discussions because of the presence of the White, heterosexual, Alpha male. Although I do not have any evidence of students feeling threatened by this male student, there were many discussions around the theme of inequity through gender norms, hyper-toxic-masculinity, race, and privilege. I observed that throughout the semester, the White male student did admit on several occasions to having a new, deeper understanding of his own privilege due to the discussions and class materials. His curious demeanor seemed to indicate a whole new perspective had opened up to him that he never knew existed. He often had many questions for his peers to better understand the complexities of realities lived by others from different sexual, racial, socio-economic, and gender identities. I interpreted this experience with the White male student as an example of the conocimiento theory in practice and witnessed by others, and myself as the students desconocimientos (not knowing, ignorance) were troubled by actively listening and engaging with his peers. By the end of the semester, his understanding of the space he fills, simply by being a White, heterosexual male in the world, became apparent through the sharing of assignments, particularly the creative poster at the culmination of the semester. His peers would joke that he was the 'token White guy' in class. In fact, this student contacted me after the semester had concluded inquiring if I would be teaching the class again or other 300 level undergraduate courses; he wrote; "I cannot take modules under 300 so I will not be joining you this semester. I hope it's a good one and you expand the consciousnesses of another heterosexual man somewhere" (January 9, 2019).

Healing

Autohistoria-teoría and conocimiento as transformative acts for empowerment can guide both students and educators through possible ways of how to reframe socially-inscribed narratives—past, present and future—toward a sense of belonging to self and in the world. Reframing embodied narratives felt by underrepresented students of not belonging on college campuses is needed to enrich society and curate education in which all can thrive (Strayhorn, 2012). The transformative acts of conocimiento are a process for healing through our wounds, teaching empathy and self-love towards wholeness.

---

[5] The Alpha and Beta male principle categorizes men into two distinct groups depending on the social traits not only in a group, but also towards the opposite sex (Sumra, 2019).

Throughout *Bridging: How Gloria Anzaldúa's Life and Work Transformed Our Own* (Keating & González-López, 2011), share how by being vulnerable, exposing and sharing their wounds, their pain, they too were able to enter a process of healing, which Anzaldúa explains through her theories. Specifically, Anzaldúa's theories of conocimiento and autohistoria-teoria invite us to cross into the difficult terrain of becoming vulnerable with self and others as a beginning to a reclusive process of healing and transformation impacting each other. Anzaldúa's innermost work of critically self-reflecting always crosses outside of herself as she made connections with others, whether through verbal sharing, art, or embodiment through writing (Keating & González-López, 2011).

Sebastián José Colón-Otero (2011) shares through prose his first encounters with Anzaldúa's words and their journey towards self-discovery and articulation of the healing process becoming activated within their life. Keating coined the term "risking the personal" to explain Anzaldúa's concept of using our lived experiences through critical self-reflection, awareness, and inner work towards healing and transformation (Keating & González-López, 2011, p. 2). Students writing, sharing, and reflecting on their own and others' testimonio is an example of the possibilities for healing as students become vulnerable with each other. For example, during the course of the semester, one of the students shared that she had to say goodbye to her grandfather, as he fell critically ill, and he passed away shortly after. Students in the class shared empathy with her as she shared her experiences and news in coping with her grandfather's loss, which also felt like losing a part of her Mexican culture and Spanish language.

The Latina/o research exercise was valuable in exposing students to an exhaustive list of Latina/o history makers in the U.S., Latin America, and the Caribbean. Most of the names and information gathered by students were new to them. For me, as an educator/curator, this assignment at the beginning of the semester was very valuable as it afforded me insight into each student and a glimpse of who they are by what they choose to highlight in their presentation. For example, one student who presented on Juan Felipe Herrera —a poet, activist, and performer, among other things —incorporated an in-depth analysis of two of Herrera's poems. The student described the style, genre, and implications of the poetry genre.

Furthermore, her analysis included comparing Herrera's work to the poets she learned about throughout her (Eurocentric) education. She explained how this unknown (to her) poet exceeded the male poets she knew, causing her to reflect on her male-poet master knowledge base thus far. She ended the presentation by paralleling one of Herrera's poems to an art piece that she admired from Basquiat. At the end of the semester, I realized that what I saw in the beginning, her love of words, poetry, and art, seeped into her work throughout the semester.

After students presented their research, there was a question and answer (Q & A) time to further the conversation. Most of the names on the list were not recognizable to students in any depth. This first assignment aided in setting a foundation of the things we do not know (desconocimientos) and questioning why the Banyan tree fruit and her roots[6] are disconnected and isolated. Discussions of colonialism, power, and privilege emerged at this point as we discussed the complexities of the U.S.'s historical involvement in Latin America and the Caribbean; and the historical and existing curations of a White supremacist educational canon in academia and public schools.

I curated a *Latina Feminisms* class art exhibit at the campus museum of art highlighting the works of Latin American/Caribbean artists from the permanent collection based on my research with Aguilar's work. The class specific art exhibit showcased the works of Ana Mendieta (Sileuta Series), Claudia Bernardi (ser mujer es resistir), and Josefina Aguilar (muñeca series). We discussed, as a class, how, when, and why artists of color and women artists are not part of mainstream art but are often tokenized and segregated. If I do not see myself represented in my local arts venue, how is that internalized pain and not-belonging felt? If I do not see others, diverse from me represented, how am I to expand my knowledge of others? Our Latina Feminisms class engaged with the artist, work, and social activism through critical reflections and discussions by curating an art exhibit specifically for students to agitate narrow definitions of multiculturalism and encourage critical self-reflection about responsibilities and accountability of institutions as collectives (Sotomayor, 2019). Introspective investigating by learners prompt their own thoughts of their values, perspectives, and beliefs as influenced by these institutions (Keating, 2007).

Interconnectedness

One of the ways in which I am interpreting interconnectedness is through student critical reflection about the testimonio shared assignment. A student wrote:

> I am grateful that my classmates felt like they could share their stories
> with me. I haven't experienced that level of depth or feeling...we were
> people who wouldn't necessarily be friends, coming to share who we

---

[6] Banyan Tree: La Ceiba, I reference in Spanish and as female because in the Spanish language it is feminine.

really are and the things we struggle with. The fact that most of us wouldn't normally be friends or even encounter one another outside of that room was actually a major advantage because I was able to open my ears to perspectives that I never would have heard before … This particular class has been the closest I have gotten to that feeling … It was a chance to exercise active listening, an open mind, and a peaceful heart … I have been able to and encouraged to do emotional work, examine myself, and pushed to grow. (G.P., October 18, 2018)

This student's experience highlights the interconnectedness by engaging in the classroom and listening to each other's testimonio. Other points of interconnectedness throughout the semester by other students included active listening, empathy, and commonality. For example, students wrote:

Hearing other people's stories made me realize to have an open mind when meeting someone. (R.C., October 13, 2018)

Transformative learning through empathy is a theme that emerged throughout the semester. One day in class, students shared about their family members who struggle with health issues and their tenuous relationship to accessing proper health care. It became apparent to me that despite students' different geographical contexts; England, Mexico, or the Northeast, they engaged through the pain of seeing someone they love enduring bodily pain and trauma and not having access to the health care needed. Students shared their reflections about interconnectedness through empath and finding similarities:

It was interesting to find out about the personal experiences that have affected everyone's lives and has enabled me to not only further understand my classmates, but also to empathize with them. (M.W., October 12, 2018)

Interconnectedness through looking for our common ground, our similarities:

I think we could severely reduce oppression and connect with people fundamentally very different[ly] than we are. For example, at first glance, it may not seem like I have much in common with some of the students in our class, simply due to differences in race and ethnicity, but we had a lot more in common due to healthcare practices and class struggles. The reality of oppression is that all types are connected, and I think that even if we cannot understand via our own lived experiences what it means to be a gender minority or a racial minority, we can empathize and come to a state of semi understanding of what that means if we can connect it to a way that we have been oppressed differently. (O.Y., October 10, 2018)

Students theorized about their own lived experiences in relation to each other and systemic oppression. Students shared their experiences of witnessing their parents battling cancer, grandparents aging and enduring health complications, and women's reproductive issues in the U.S., signaling to us as a class that although our contexts differ, many core systems of power remain in place.

Not belonging: Autohistoria-teoría

Anzaldúa challenges preconceived notions of the categorization of theory and its historical lineage. Her holistic theoretical approach towards transformation and social change pivots from critical self-reflection, self-change, and a transformative process of healing through conocimiento (Keating & González-López, 2011). Anzaldúa's theorizing pioneered a new way of knowing and feminist knowledge building that emerges through the body or lived experiences from historically *othered* bodies. She writes, "[w]hat is considered theory in the dominant academic community is not necessarily what counts as theory for women-of-color"; her quote further explains that teorías are needed to understand new methods of knowing specifically situated in our own lived experiences that have been historically invisible (Anzaldúa, 1990, p. xxv). In the introduction to the second edition of *Borderlands* (Anzaldúa, 1999), Sonia Saldívar-Hull (1999) wrote:

> In 1991, Héctor Calderòn and José Saldívar published the groundbreaking anthology, *Criticism in the Borderland: Studies in Chicano Literature, Culture and Ideology*. Emily Hicks published *Border Writing: The Multidimensional Text* (1991), and Ruth Bear crossed generic and disciplinary borders in her study, *Translated Woman: Crossing the Border with Esperanza's Story* in 1993. (p. 12)

Saldívar noted other significant work, too, including Alfred Arteaga's (1994) anthology, *Another Tongue: National and Ethnicity in the Linguistic Borderlands* (Eoyang, Niranjana, & Lloyd, 1994); Carl Gutiérrez-Jones (1995), *Rethinking the Borderlands*; and Guillermo Gómez-Peña (1996), *The New World Border*.

The feelings of not belonging that I felt throughout the semester were doubting my knowledge and ability to facilitate the class. I did not feel like this with every class taught, but in some particular situations I did. For example, one of the identity poems shared by a male identifying student was about an incident he had years prior. He had been at the wrong place at the wrong time, and was both part of and victim of a violent male group physical fight that sent him to the hospital with severe wounds. His takeaway, as he shared, from his experience that night was that he felt he always needs to be vigilant and physically fit to be prepared for any violent situation that may occur. I felt conflicted about his narrative. I wasn't sure how to engage with it. On one hand I felt that his experience was a reflection of hyper-masculinity, violence, and trauma. On the other hand he, as a member of a dominant group in society, I felt a keen awareness to the 'space' he took up in the class. Was this his male privilege and ego boosting of a patriarchal system in the flesh? How were the other students feeling about this? Does anyone in the class feel threatened by him? I felt uncomfortable, and I felt that some students did as well.

We continued class by opening it up for discussion after his sharing of his identity poem. As the students continued to discuss the male student's poem, asking questions, and digging a bit more, the conversations revealed that there were layers of mental health, emotional, and relational issues that he began to notice and work on because of his experience that night after a fight outside a club. He also became aware of the life track he was on, and he needed to make changes, realizing that his vulnerabilities were also strengths, places to grow. The experience of my feeling uncomfortable and not quite knowing how to continue but trusting the process of actively listening and intentional in finding common threads with each other, was a powerful one.

Autohistoria-teoría at its core is individuals who have felt excluded, silenced, and invisible have the power, necessity, to create new ways of thinking which center around their own experiences. Touching on the contradictions being felt simultaneously of not belonging and belonging, one student wrote, "I felt connected to Juan and Silvia, despite not being Latina, because they talked about struggling with their identities and with their families, but also celebrating them" (10/13/18).

Anzaldúa writes that women of color are often forced to wear masks, and it isn't until we begin to crack the mask and pry it off of our faces that one's own identity is made through theorizing about lived experiences (Anzaldúa, 1990). I witnessed the beginning of a theory-in-the-making with a student who identified as Mexican American, who came to class and shared sporadically throughout the semester. When she did share, it was a sharing of vulnerable subjects as they related to her Mexican-American identity. She explains, "I have to say in my college experience so far, I've felt really distant from the school and my peers for a lot of reasons. Whenever I came to your class I always felt comfortable with the people around me and it was a really eye opening experience to hear everyone's experiences in their lives and meet other [L]atinx community members as well" (December 2018). This same student wrote me an email after the semester had ended, disclosing how the course had given her awareness and enhanced her college trajectory. She wrote: "I'm happy to say that I ended up choosing to major in Spanish with a minor in Latino/a studies! Without this class I don't think I ever would've had that in my considerations before." Without a letter from this particular student, I don't think I would have necessarily known the positive impact and transformative learning that the course had on her because of her overall reserved nature in class. More significant with the purpose of this teacher inquiry, she felt the sense of not belonging in the 'college setting' and took steps to become aware of her Mexican roots and transform her education in creating her own narrative. She wrote, "I haven't enjoyed a lot of aspects of my college career so far and often feel like maybe I don't belong in the college setting but this class always gave me the motivation."

On the subjects of privilege and challenging oppressive systems, another student shared in her critical reflection blog how her feelings *of* belonging made her aware of her privileges, and difference was celebrated, not challenged. She writes:

> Challenging beliefs is something that I want to do, but never seem to be able to do. I wonder if this actually comes from a place of privilege, i.e., I have never had to challenge social norms because I have always fit right in, and when I didn't fit in, my differences were praised as a strength rather than weakness. This privilege is something that I need to be more aware of in my daily life (W. E., September 20, 2018)

I had another Latina student who went beyond the creative poster final project presentation by creating a timeline of her life thus far (21 years) as her autohistoria and testimonio. Throughout the presentation of her timeline, she explained how she hadn't realized how much living in-between cultures and feelings of not belonging had impacted her life, identity, and competitive work ethic as a woman of color, and how they continue to today. This student's example is one that brings us back to the Banyan tree—feeling disconnected and a sense of not belonging. She expressed how her feelings of isolation in predominantly White and sexist environments made her feel a deep sense of not belonging as a Latina woman. Her tenacity drove her to end up in an engineering major that was White male-dominated, where she continuously felt "in a different world," which felt incredibly difficult to navigate.

Healing through our wounds: Conocimiento

The transformative acts of the conocimiento theory is a process of healing, "surrendering the self, sacrificing a certain way of being, you go through the whole process again, repeating all seven stages of the cycle" (Anzaldúa, 2015, p. 142). Healing through our wounds from colonialism, discrimination, or trauma, individually or collectively, causes our fragmentation and needing holism of the body, spirit and mind. Like the Coyolxauhqui imperative, taking the fragments of our life and putting ourselves together is healing through our wounds in search of "inner completeness" (Anzaldúa, 2009, p. 320). Vallone (2014) writes that the healing of wounds does not stop at wholeness, but also needs reparation. Vallone explains that conscious awareness is only part of the process towards wholeness because public acknowledgment and taking responsibility are just as important. She writes, "[n]ot just healing, but having the wounds acknowledged publicly" (Vallone, 2014, p. 32). By taking responsibility and public acknowledgment, Vallone (2014) is connecting Anzaldúa's (2015) pivotal point of interconnectedness—we are all impacted by each other.

Using Anzaldúa's theories of conocimiento and autohistoria-teoría in this curated process-oriented approach for experiencing the transformative acts of conocimiento, learners explored and identified the impact of their dislocation. Like the pollinating which occurs inside the Banyan tree, "[t]o be in conocimiento with someone or some group is to pool resources, share knowledge, and do the work of repairing the wounds" (Anzaldúa, 2015, p. 234). As seen in Anzaldúa's work, wounds and vulnerability is a large part of the transformative process of healing and meaning-making (Vallone, 2014). For example, one student describes healing through storytelling as a form of changing oneself with agency, she writes:

> I am a storyteller, but I am coming to terms with it. I'm not a writer. I don't have the attention span to sit and create worlds and people on paper. But I've been making them up in my head ever since I can remember. I remember being very young and sitting in front of my bathroom mirror. I would play songs on my radio and act them out for myself. Trying to contort my face in pain well enough to play Fantine in *Les Misérables*, I began to feel differently. The fact that I could change myself into someone else gave me the ability to get through tough times as I was growing up. I believe what Anzaldúa says about healing through storytelling. Every new story changes you and gives you a new tool, or even a coping mechanism. (I. L., November 4, 2018)

Another student recalls a version of her former self that has since dissipated. She is reminded of the commune of her spiritual and physical body through la facultad when we read chapter 3, "Entering the Serpent." I interpret her awakening of cultivating her neglected self with her body and spirit to the healing of wounds through la facultad as a holistic practice of reuniting spirit and body. Like the germinating seeds of the Banyan tree from the inside, a transformation begins to take a form that may not be visible.

> Gradually my outlook shifted to become generally more oblivious to what I was once very sensitive to. The value in cultivating la facultad, I now realize, is returning to spiritual peace and returning to my body. (Y.O., October 9, 2018)

Next, one student connects Audre Lorde's concept of self-preservation to Anzaldúa's symbol of Coatlicue (the third transformative act in the conocimiento theory) and draws a parallel to the trauma of her lived experiences and making new meaning from pain. She explains:

> Audre Lord said that "caring for myself is not self-indulgence. It is self-preservation, and that is an act of political warfare." I think that Coatlicue is about "taking back" what has traumatized you and permitting it to make you "better" somehow. In my own personal experience, I don't think I would be who I am today without the trauma I have experienced. My abusive alcoholic father taught me that I am strong enough to walk away. My psychologically abusive stepfather taught me how to be empathetic and how to carry a much larger emotional burden than I think the average person is capable of (I'm working through that right now, but could I be as "nice" or "understanding" as everyone says I am if I didn't deal with this pain as a child? I don't think so). (E.K., September 18, 2018)

Another critical reflection from a student's blog post discusses what I conclude to be describing a form of healing through our wounds. The student writes her critical self-reflection after a class discussion. They explain how empathy and vulnerability can "bridge the gap" of traumas experienced by recognizing our commonalities, our interconnectedness of being hurt and in pain. The conocimiento process has the precursor of vulnerability implicitly within it— facilitating pain and wounds to come out of the shadows and become a "powerful agent of transformation," allowing for interconnectedness and empowerment (Vallone, 2014, p. 40). The student wrote:

I really think that trauma is undefinable. No one experiences it in the same light, in the same way, under the same circumstances. But I think empathy can bridge that gap between individual trauma. Listening to people's stories today, their pain and their hurt, made me feel my own empathy towards them. But more importantly, it made me believe in the empathy in others. I believe in energy, as zany as it sounds, I think people feel differently, and the energy of a group can have the power to change your mood and your life. And to experience the energy of the room today was really special. It is not often in daily life that people appear vulnerable. We build up walls to get through the day, and we perfect our "public persona," who we are when the cameras are rolling. So to see people express emotion in tandem with other human beings was refreshing, even revitalizing after a long week of bottling feelings and setting them aside. (I. S., October 8, 2018)

Akin to a Shaman, who works *with* the wound *not against* it to find a way to reveal and heal on a spiritual level; healing through our wounds is a radical holistic act in theorizing our lived experiences, challenging dominant societal views (Facio & Lara, 2014).

Conclusions and implications

Curating an educational space using Anzaldúa's theories of conocimiento and autohistoria-teoría allowed me to create a rich environment where the learners and I built community through interconnections and cultivated our inner voice. By internalizing testimonio both conceptually and theoretically, I established the feminist curatorial pillars of awakening, vulnerability, wandering, healing, and interconnectedness. Establishing these pillars is a journey that I am only beginning. I considered the implications of what I had learned about the process-oriented decolonial feminist teaching approach, and I came to these conclusions: We are more similar than different as human beings, and we (as people) are not broken, but whole and waiting to embody who we really are. Furthermore, in critically reflecting on the human condition, we come into our own, finding authentic ways of embodying wholeness.

My pedagogy is informed by an epistemology of testimonios: a strong sense that our being in the world has a lot to do with our knowing in the world. Ruth Trinidad Galván (2016) explains that many Chicana and Latina feminists have intentionally broken away from Western thinking and logic in order to validate and remember their cultural knowledge. For many Chicanas and Latinas, cultural memory is deeply rooted in a history of oppression and colonization in the United States and their home countries (Elenes, 2011). The struggle to remember ancestral knowledge (Anzaldúa, 1999) and decolonize the mind, body, soul, and spirit requires an understanding of the underpinnings of epistemic power (Mignolo, 2005).

Students shared their final creative poster projects during the last week of the semester: creative manifestations of the beginnings of their own autohistoria-teorías. As they shared their projects, many of the students became emotional, as they were giving voice to many parts of their identities and lived experiences for the first time. Students explained how the class had changed their lives because they understood themselves better now (16 weeks later) and had a new perspective on their parents' experiences and origins. At the very least, the students had had inspiring conversations with the people they love. I believe that at the core of autohistoria-teoría and conocimiento, as well as the search for our authentic selves, is the process by which we become *real*. The masks start to fall away. The shallow responses deepen. Our interactions with others become more profound because we are learning how to be present, vulnerable, and reflective. Because we know that we are all interconnected in some way. Because I was able to be real, authentic with my students as I facilitated conversations that in turn allowed them, invited them, to be real, too. My pedagogical approach to curricular development and the curation of the educational environment encouraged learners to question, critically reflect on, and create meaning from their lived experiences and interactions in the world (Galván, 2016).

Curating is both a concept and an action. Curating involves suturing together narratives, symbols, and visions and breathing them into being in the world. Creative expressions, or acts, are processes of "(ad)venturing into the inner void, extrapolating meaning from it and sending it out into the world"—a holistic experience (Anzaldúa & Keating, 2005, p. 275). Curating, curando, invites a new definition of self that incorporates autonomy. A new definition of success that is anchored in the spiritual activism from within.

Critical reflections

Curating a feminist college course is a creative methodology in which the body is both the form and site for making meaning through creative writing, art-making, performing, dancing, healing, teaching, meditating, and spiritualizing (Anzaldúa & Keating, 2009). The body of the curator/educator/learner becomes a site for manifesting creative acts through the conocimiento process as consciousness is awakened, evoked. The experiences that Anzaldúa (2015) describes as shamanic shapeshifting are the catalyst for becoming a vessel, a site for creativity. My body became a site for creativity through the curation of the *Latina Feminisms* course, my facilitation and mediation of the classroom environment, and my interactions with my students. The site of creativity is considered a transformative act in conocimiento theory because it is constantly changing throughout the spiral of life; with each crossing, new perspective, and awakening, transformation is occurring.

In this study, curation was a creative knowledge-building process that involved the gathering of perspectives expressed through visual art, writing, and performance, among other forms. Curation also involved critical self-reflection and making meaning from these perspectives as they connect to a collective body. In curating an undergraduate classroom space and syllabus, working through "psychic unrest" is essential. The experience of unrest and rupture by both the educator/curator and learners allows creative acts (e.g., reflective writing, art-making, poetry, music, and testimonios) to manifest. Anzaldúa (2009) explains such crossings as border art crossings that endure rupture, fragmentation and are active sites for resistance.

My experience engaging with feminist writing, active listening and self-disclosure in the form of testimonio was an act of vulnerability as I suture fragments together. The process-oriented feminist teaching approach I used for curating an environment and curriculum facilitated opportunities for dialogue, historical contextualization, and the validation of individual lived experiences coming together as a collective. Overall there were many positive takeaways from the *Latina Feminisms* curriculum. I had the opportunity of curating the course around my own research interests, areas of strength, and my own experience and understanding of the needs of young learners. It was apparent to me that the class came together as a space for sharing, vulnerability, and healing. Students shared deeply personal experiences such as trauma, violence, death, and mental health issues. The Banyan tree does not need to bloom to show off its flower; it blooms on the inside for itself.

Curatorial challenges

There were several challenges I encountered throughout the semester that further merit consideration. For example, the emotional labor of intentionally curating an approach for the healing and self-empowerment of underserved and underrepresented learners can be taxing. Intentionally curating spaces for deep-dive vulnerability through testimonios is work. Everyone in the space needs to share; this is not necessarily an option but rather the essence of coming together. This may be challenging for some as it is often a new experience within academic spaces. For others, it may come easy, and the platform may entice some to engage with the class session as a therapy session; this is not the point of feminist curating in educational spaces. Rather, it is the place to share as an equitable place of listening and sharing, not monopolizing discussions for personal gain only. In these spaces, there must be a willingness to accept emotional discomfort as participation in experiences of internalized oppression is communicated. My hope is that in curating feminist educational spaces, compassion, kindness, and respect are strengthened as a valuable moral ethic to build feminist testimonial curated educational spaces. For this reason, it is crucial for curators to be prepared to affirm learners' vulnerability as they express emotions that often emerge as a result of speaking what was previously invisible (Mendez-Negrete, 2013). One of the ways I affirmed learners' voices was by making sure each learner shared in the space.

Because we, as curators and facilitators, are aware and awakened in many ways and have, more often than not, had our own painful experiences and struggles throughout academia and feelings of not belonging. I want to be there for students emotionally because we know how it feels to be isolated, alone. Self-care is thus a significant part of curating educational environments for healing our wounds. Having boundaries for the work is important. I developed boundaries for myself as I was navigating these issues with students. I had students who came to me because of relationship violence, depression, mental health, physical health, and personal life circumstances that were beyond their control. I wanted to help everyone. I decided to build my community with resources and people I knew and trusted. I brought these people into the classroom for workshops, made information available to students both digitally and in class, and personally directed students to resources and helped them determine what they needed to do. However, the work that I am describing is a lot of emotional labor: touching base with students, following up with students, putting students in contact with resources. Creating a community of fantastic people and resources was a huge support to my students and me. But it also meant that I needed my own needs met so as not to become depleted.

Healing

As I reflect, I realize that there were moments throughout the semester when I felt incredibly moved emotionally by students' voices as they shared of themselves. At times I felt it was difficult to engage in conversations because of my own lived experiences; I, too, am engaged in a healing process. In one instance, in particular, I had a guest speaker come in to share information about domestic violence, and I realized that I was relieved that she was facilitating the conversation because it would have been too hard for me. As a facilitator for the class, if I had not been in a place of self-empowerment and healing, it would have been impossible to create an intimate, safe environment as I moved through my own pain and wounds with my students.

The sensitivity of many of the issues discussed throughout the semester and students' deeply reflective reactions like entries of student connections to domestic violence and abuse made me aware of the need to address this sensitivity in greater detail in the future. Addressing potential trigger points and themes that may be uncomfortable and difficult to navigate early on in these educational spaces made the students aware of an emotional cost they would most likely bear and is important and bears deep consideration. As an educator/curator, how will one deal with uncomfortable topics? Vulnerable confessions? One's own emotional responses? I believe that discomfort is permissible and necessary to critically reflect and become vulnerable within the boundaries of the educational spaces. Dialogue produces empathy and new ways of imagining future narratives.

Well-being is important, especially since the students tackle challenging topics with strong emotional and psychological resonances. I recommend implementing "pit stops" to address mindfulness and self-care at the beginning or end of each class. Perhaps including simple self-assessment questions that the students and educator can end/begin with or meditate/journal on would bring attention to our own bodies and selves: What we are feeling and why? We cannot have empathy towards others if we do not love ourselves first. Some questions might be: Why am I sharing this? What outcome am I hoping for?

What am I feeling? What are my intentions? Do they align with my values? Is there an outcome that will hurt my feelings? Am I being honest with myself? Am I taking something personally? Am I doing my best?

I found that the students and I often brought in more supporting materials each week to better articulate potential meanings as we navigated *Borderlands* (1999). Because the course emphasized dialogue and participation, I welcomed sources of further inquiry that are relevant to each person's lived experience. For example, I have had some students share readings, music, poetry, art, and podcasts that resonated with their lived experiences and connected to broader collective themes in class.

Since I was advocating for a position of the most equality possible, a position in which we are all vulnerable to each other, I could not be merely a spectator. I was the last one to share my testimonio. I considered what I would share, what might be too personal, what might be considered questionable within the context of the student/instructor relationship, even if I did not see it that way. I realize that throughout my teaching, I share about my personal lived experiences as I teach; it is a thread embedded in who I am and how I approach relationships with my art, curating and as an educator. I do not see how I could segregate aspects of my life as I teach; I see them all as interconnected. Furthermore, I do not feel that I can advocate for vulnerable educational spaces towards transformation and healing if I am unwilling to do the work I am requesting from my students. I firmly believe I must model in myself first what I desire to build with others in the world.

I realized my position in teaching in the past was one of opposition, which is contrary to what I desired in theory, that of a non-oppositional lens. I believe that there is great merit in feeling discomfort and critically reflecting, looking inward, and navigating difficult waters with ourselves and others. However, I realized that creating or framing a class environment from the lens of opposing sides is not what I intend or desire. I had to intentionally navigate the course by supplementing readings and offering some dialogic questions to prompt students to consider how we are similar. For example, how is the idea of race constructed? How does the social construction of race and performative gender identity roles shape different populations of people globally? In questioning and unpacking these large themes as a collective, students and I were able to see how we have all been impacted in disenfranchising ways. At times I felt conflicted about realizing that my practice as an educator/curator was actually one of opposition in many ways. As I reflect on my teaching, it becomes clear that my premise often was about what wasn't present, accessible, or facilitated within institutional systems, the internalized oppressions. I find myself wrestling with this frequently. I realize that deeper critical self-reflection and analysis of the social constructions of intersectionalities help to set the stage for many of our consequential conversations. Examining the construction of internalized systemic oppression may have helped create a shared foundation of knowledge among the students, wherein they could use the same language and lens. Yes, we were specifically discussing Latinas in the United States, but showing how internalized systemic oppression functions on various levels affecting various groups of people helped me avoid reducing oppression to just a "race" issue but rather a larger system and framework at work.

I think that an important part of this feminist curatorial, educational approach is connecting to creative acts in diverse ways that connect with each learner. For example, as an artist, if I am engaging with my painting art and Anzaldúa's theory, I feel it is a strong connection that organically is enacted within me. At the beginning of the semester, I am intentional in understanding and helping the learner identify what creative act they are naturally drawn to (writing, poetry, sculpture, etc.) and using that creative act as a vehicle for their autohistoria-teoría. In my experience as a learner, artist, and educator, as time progresses, the learner will begin to realize that they are theorizing about their lived experience through their work.

Implications for art education

As I reflect on the journey thus far as a learner, artist, curator and educator, I am writing this manuscript in the midst of continued intensified upheaval in our U.S. nation. We continue to witness brown and black bodies murdered before us, injustices so vile that perhaps now, in 2020, White complacency is being challenged more deeply than ever before. Racism and white privilege have led to deep trauma and pain, situated within U.S. historical contexts of institutionalized oppression in the arts, education and beyond. Historically and contemporarily, museums, gallery and educational spaces have predominantly been White environments with White gatekeepers who have not been forcefully anti-racist as organizations. Moving forward, I believe that we each have a responsibility to engage with many of these social issues and conversations with action. Token representations and curriculum are not enough; it never was enough. Adding diverse individuals into the curriculum is not enough. Engaging in uncomfortable conversations to impact transformation, healing, and awakening is necessary. Education models in the U.S. have not transformed adequately, in my opinion. The stories that I repeatedly hear from students in high school and college classrooms, unfortunately, remind me of my own experiences that are racist and marginalizing. To critically assess and be honest with ourselves as educators, artists and curators is hard work with hard truths.

This approach to curating feminist educational spaces contributes to the existing scholarship of Latina/os in the arts and education, particularly Chicana and Latina explorations of decolonizing knowledge production. In examining underserved learners and their undergraduate experiences, paradigms of whiteness within institutions towards healing from educational trauma and challenging oppressive systems of education may be addressed through conocimiento theory in practice. Applying conocimiento theory allows educators to expand the current breadth of scholarship through critical reflection and consciousness.

A process-oriented feminist teaching approach to curating a classroom environment and curriculum is interdisciplinary (Murillo, Villenas, Galván, Muñoz, Martínez, & Machado-Casas, 2009). The *Latina Feminisms* course attracted students from various fields, and naturally, these learners contributed knowledge from not only their lived experiences but also from their home disciplines. I highly encouraged students to intentionally connect with their majors/minors and consider how they could apply what we discussed and learned to their fields.

I critically reflected on a process-oriented feminist teaching approach to art. In particular, I showed how I curated the curriculum for the *Latina Feminisms* course with the objective of decolonizing academic canons. Scholarship often excludes underrepresented learners and their histories, causing students to feel a deep sense of not belonging. An educator who values and validates each learner's experiences, or well of knowledge, creates an environment that says, "You matter, your voice matters." I believe that learners can be what we encourage them to imagine. If I create an environment that offers space for sharing and acknowledging learners' lived experiences as places of information and meaningful knowledge, then eventually, with time, I think the learners may also believe that about themselves. Experiential knowledge is a seed. In my journey so far, I have had many voices encourage and support me, seeing what I could not see in myself. Because others had expectations of me, for me, I found my purpose in rising to meet the expectations and in that process, I became empowered.

Who should or could teach a *Latina Feminisms* course? Teaching a course such as *Latina Feminisms* requires an educator to have particular attributes. First, the educator should be able to recognize and analyze power and privilege and have a hyper-awareness of power dynamics in any given situation or environment. Secondly, the educator should critically reflect on their own positionality as individuals and as part of a collective embodiment. Thirdly, the educator should be able to challenge binary thinking and analysis as a way of blurring traditional models and narrow thinking. Fourthly, the educator should use mindfulness through spiritual activism as a guidepost in curating an environment where intimacy and vulnerability thrive; the educator should care deeply about issues of social justice and transformation from the personal to the political and collective. I define mindfulness as a deep awareness that is intuitive and spiritual.

I think that this curatorial approach can open possibilities to many potential iterations and is appropriate for many disciplines, including education, sociology, history, Caribbean and Latin American studies, African/Latino/Chicano studies, and art education. In my experience as a student, the required coursework is often limited to U.S. contexts that are narrowly defined through White, Eurocentric paradigms. Despite the many of my peers coming from diverse backgrounds outside of the United States. Integrating layers of richness by inviting other ways of thinking and theorizing through testimonio and autohistoria-teoría has the potential to open up interdisciplinary research and scholarship and welcome new possibilities that are far beyond Eurocentric paradigms. What would happen if educators curated undergraduate courses in such a way that testimonios comprised the curricula? Where spiritual activism was a way of doing, making, creating, and practicing art and education? Where the whole person is validated and respected instead of compartmentalizing parts of who we are?

I also recognize the contradictions and difficulties of navigating these spaces. I am constantly reminded of the caution that decolonization should not be a metaphor for social justice initiatives (Tuck & Yang, 2012) because of the reality that our U.S. country was stolen from Indigenous peoples setting forth a paradigm of settler-native-slave that still exists contemporarily. We, as a country, have not shed our history; we intentionally reproduce it as part of our power framework in how we move and operate in the world. This dark realization is one that must be confronted. I initiate dislocation intentionally via curriculum curation as a jarring experience questioning the cultural and social narratives we have been taught to consume.

Curating educational spaces that value university experience with lived experiences as participatory spaces for community learning and knowledge sharing and building. Educators need to explore and develop New pedagogical strategies needed for engagement and action. This is not only for the learner's well-being but also for the educators. Educators are often overworked, overwhelmed and undervalued; how then, I ask, can empowering transformational stewardship for knowledge building occur if the very pillars of our educational structures are being crushed under the burden? I firmly believe that I cannot facilitate feminist educational spaces if I myself am not committed to the hard emotional and spiritual labor required to be present and engage with others through compassion, integrity and respect.

References

Alarcón, N. (1983). Chicana's feminist literature: A re-vision through Malintzin/or Malintzin: Putting flesh back on the object. In C. Moraga & G. Anzaldúa (Eds.), *This bridge called my back: Writings by radical women of color* (2nd ed.) (pp. 182–190). Latham, NY: Kitchen Table, Women of Color Press.

Alcoff, L. M. (2005). *Visible identities: Race, gender, and the self.* Oxford, United Kingdom: Oxford University Press.

Anzaldúa, G. (Ed.). (1990). *Making face, making soul: Haciendo caras: Creative and critical perspectives by feminists of color* (1st ed.). San Francisco, CA: Aunt Lute Books.

Anzaldúa, G. (1999). *Borderlands: La frontera: The new mestiza* (2nd ed.). San Francisco, CA: Aunt Lute Books.

Anzaldúa, G. (2015). *Light in the dark: Luz en lo Oscuro: Rewriting identity, spirituality, reality.* A. Keating, Ed. Durham, NC: Duke University Press.

Anzaldúa, G., & Keating, A. (2009). *The Gloria Anzaldúa reader.* Durham, NC: Duke University Press.

Anzaldúa, G., & Keating, A. (Eds.). (2002). *This bridge we call home: Radical visions for transformation.* New York, NY: Routledge.

Ayala, C. (2001). From sugar plantations to military bases: The U.S. Navy's expropriations in Vieques, Puerto Rico, 1940–45. *Centro: Journal of the Center for Puerto Rican Studies, 13*(1), 22–44.

Barber, M. J. (2010). *How the Irish, Germans, and Czechs became Anglo: Race and identity in the Texas-Mexico borderlands* [Unpublished doctoral dissertation]. University of Texas at Austin.

Behar, R. (1996). *The vulnerable observer: Anthropology that breaks your heart.* Boston, MA: Beacon Press.

Behar, R. (2013). *Traveling heavy.* Durham, NC: Duke University Press.

Behar, R., & Gordon, D. A. (Eds.). (1995). *Women writing culture.* Berkeley, CA: University of California Press.

Betts, R. (2012). Decolonization: A brief history of the word. In E. Bogarteas & R. Raben (Eds.), *Beyond empire and nation: The decolonization of African and Asian societies, 1930s–1970s* (pp. 23–38). Leiden, Netherlands: Brill.

Bhattacharya, K. (2013). Performing gender as "Third-World-Other" in higher education: De/colonizing transnational feminist possibilities. *Creative Approaches to Research, 6*(3), 30–43.

Bhattacharya, K., & Keating, A. (2018). Expanding beyond public and private realities: Evoking Anzaldúan autohistoria-teoría in two voices. *Qualitative Inquiry, 24*(5), 345–354.

Bhattacharya, K., & Payne, R. (2016). Mixing mediums, mixing selves: Arts-based contemplative approaches to border crossings. *International Journal of Qualitative Studies in Education, 29*(9), 1100–1117.

Bosco, F. J. (2006). The Madres de Plaza de Mayo and three decades of human rights activism: Embeddedness, emotions, and social movements. *Annals of the Association of American Geographers, 96*(2), 342–365.

Collins, P. H. (2008). Reply to commentaries: Black sexual politics revisited. *Studies in Gender and Sexuality, 9*(1), 68–85.

Collins, P. J. (2002). Connecting anthropology and Quakerism: Transcending the insider/outsider dichotomy. In E. Arweck and M. D. Stringer (Eds.), *Theorizing faith: The insider/outsider problem in the study of ritual* (pp. 77–95). Birmingham: University of Birmingham Press.

Colón-Otero, S. J. (2011). Anzaldúa, Maestra. In A. Keating & G. González-López (Eds.), *Bridging: How Gloria Anzaldúa's life and work transformed our own* (pp. 65–67). Austin, TX: University of Texas Press.

Comaroff, J., & Comaroff, J. L. (2015). *Theory from the South: Or, how Euro-America is evolving toward Africa.* New York, NY: Routledge.

Connell, R. (2014). Using southern theory: Decolonizing social thought in theory, research and application. *Planning Theory, 13*(2), 210–223.

Cosden, M., & Newman, B. (2015). *Edison and Ford in Florida (Images of America).* Mt. Pleasant, SC: Arcadia Publishing.

Creary, N. M. (Ed.). (2012). *African intellectuals and decolonization.* Columbus, OH: Ohio University Press.

Crenshaw, K. (1989). *Demarginalizing the intersection of race and sex: A black feminist critique of antidiscrimination doctrine, feminist theory and antiracist politics.* Chicago, IL: University of Chicago Legal Foundations.

D'Alessandro, M. (1998). Los movimientos sociales en la transición democrática. El caso de las Madres de Plaza de Mayo: sentimiento y discurso. *América Latina Hoy, 20.*

Dana, N. F., & Yendol-Hoppey, D. (2014). *The reflective educator's guide to classroom research: Learning to teach and teaching to learn through practitioner inquiry* (3rd. ed.). Chicago, IL: Corwin Press.

David, E. J. R. (Ed.). (2013). *Internalized oppression: The psychology of marginalized groups.* New York, NY: Springer.

de Onís, C. M. (2017). What's in an "x"?: An exchange about the politics of "Latinx." *Chiricù Journal: Latina/o Literature, Art, and Culture, 1*(2), 78–91.

Desai, D. (2019). Cultural diversity in art education. In K. Freedman (Ed.), *The international encyclopedia of art and design education* (vol. 2) (pp. 1–21). Hoboken, NJ: John Wiley & Sons Ltd.

Du Bois, W. E. B. (2006). Double-consciousness and the veil. In R. F. Levine (Ed.), *Social class and stratification: Classic statements and theoretical debates* (pp. 203–277). Oxford: Rowman & Littlefield.

Duran, E. (2013). Forward. In E. J. R. David (Ed.), *Internalized oppression: The psychology of marginalized groups* (pp. xiii–xvii). New York, NY: Springer Publishing Company.

Eeds, M., & Peterson, R. (1991). Teacher as curator: Learning to talk about literature. *Reading Teacher, 45*(2), 118–126.

Elenes, A. (2011). *Transforming borders: Chicana/O popular culture and pedagogy.* New York, NY: Lexington Books.

Eoyang, E., Niranjana, T., & Lloyd, D. (1994). *Another tongue: Nation and ethnicity in the linguistic borderlands.* Durham, NC: Duke University Press.

Facio, E., & Lara, I. (Eds.) (2014). *Fleshing the spirit: Spirituality and activism in Chicana, Latina, and Indigenous women's lives.* Tucson, AZ: University of Arizona Press.

Firmat, G. P. (2012). *Life on the hyphen: The Cuban-American way.* Austin, TX: University of Texas Press.

Font, M., & Quiroz, A. (Eds.). (2006). *The Cuban Republic and José Martí: Reception and use of a national symbol.* Lanham, MD: Lexington Books.

Freire, P. (1970). *Pedagogy of the oppressed.* New York, NY: Herder & Herder.

Gaxiola Serrano, T. J., González Ybarra, M., & Delgado Bernal, D. (2019). "Defend yourself with words, with the knowledge that you've gained": An exploration of conocimiento among Latina undergraduates in ethnic studies. *Journal of Latinos and Education, 18*(3), 243–257.

Gómez-Peña, G. (1996). *The New World border: Prophecies, poems, & loqueras for the end of the century.* San Francisco, CA: City Lights.

Greene, M. (1978). *Landscapes of learning.* New York, NY: Teachers College Press.

Greene, M. (1995). Art and imagination: Reclaiming the sense of possibility. *Phi Delta Kappan, 76*(5), 378–382.

Gutiérrez-Jones, C. (1995). *Rethinking the borderlands: Between Chicano culture and legal discourse* (vol. 4). Oakland, CA: University of California Press.

Herrera, A. O. R. (2011). *Cuban artists across the diaspora: Setting the tent against the house.* Austin, TX: University of Texas Press.

History. (2021). Taíno Museum. https://tainomuseum.org/taino/history/

Hurtado, A. (2003). Theory in the flesh: Toward an endarkened epistemology. *International Journal of Qualitative Studies in Education, 16*(2), 215–225.

Hurtado, S., & Carter, D. F. (1997). Effects of college transition and perceptions of the campus racial climate on Latino college students' sense of belonging. *Sociology of Education, 70*(4), 324–345.

Introduction: Caney Circle. (n.d.). https://caneycircle.wordpress.com/intro/

Irwin, R. L., Beer, R., Springgay, S., Grauer, K., Xiong, G., & Bickel, B. (2006). The rhizomatic relations of a/r/tography. *Studies in Art Education, 48*(1), 70–88.

Jacoby, B. (2010). How can I promote deep learning through critical reflection? *Magna Publications.* http://www.magnapubs.com/mentor-commons/?video=25772a92#.UjnHBazD-70

Johnson, R. B., & Christensen, L. (2019). *Educational research: Quantitative, qualitative, and mixed approaches.* Los Angeles, CA: Sage Publications.

Jung, C. G. (2014). *Collected works of C. G. Jung* (Vol. 9, Part 1: Archetypes and the collective unconscious) (2nd ed.). G. Adler & R. F. C. Hull, Trans. Princeton, NJ: Princeton University Press.

Kaufman, G. (1992). *Shame: The power of caring.* Rochester, VA: Schenkman Books.

Keating, A. (2005). *EntreMundos/AmongWorlds: New perspectives on Gloria E. Anzaldúa.* New York, NY: Springer.

Keating, A. (2006). From borderlands and new mestizas to nepantlas and nepantleras: Anzaldúan theories for social change. *Human Architecture: Journal of the Sociology of Self-knowledge, 4*(3), 3–12.

Keating, A. (2007). *Teaching transformation: Transcultural classroom dialogues.* New York, NY: Springer.

Keating, A., & González-López, G. (2011). *Bridging: How Gloria Anzaldúa's life and work transformed our own.* Austin, TX: University of Texas Press.

Keifer-Boyd, K. (2014). Feminist perspectives. In K. Miraglia & C. Smilan (Eds.), *Inquiry in action: Paradigms, methodologies and perspectives in art education research* (pp. 193–203). Reston, VA: The National Art Education Association.

Keifer-Boyd, K. (2019). Cultures of curriculum. In K. Freedman (Ed.), *The international encyclopedia of art and design education* (Vol. 2: Curricular aspects of art & design education) (pp. 75--85). Hoboken, NJ: John Wiley & Sons Ltd.

Klein, C. F. (2008). A new interpretation of the Aztec statue called Coatlicue, "Snakes-Her-Skirt." *Ethnohistory, 55*(2), 229–250.

Knight, W. B. (2006). E(raced) bodies in and out of sight/cite/site. *Journal of Social Theory in Art Education, 26*, 323–342.

Knight, W. B. (2007). Entangled social realities: Race, class, and gender—A triple threat to the academic achievement of Black females. *Visual Culture & Gender, 2*, 24–38.

Koshy, K. (2006). Nepantlera-activism in the transnational moment: In dialogue with Gloria Anzaldúa's theorizing of nepantla. *Human Architecture: Journal of the Sociology of Self-Knowledge, 4*(3), 147–161.

Laman, T. G. (1995). The ecology of strangler fig seedling establishment. *Selbyana, 16*(2), 223–229.

Lippard, L. R. (1990). *Mixed blessings: New art in a multicultural America.* New York, NY: Pantheon Books.

Lockhart, T. (2006). Writing the self: Gloria Anzaldúa, textual form, and feminist epistemology. *Michigan Feminist Studies, 20*(1), 1–11.

Lugones, M. (2010). Toward a decolonial feminism. *Hypatia, 25*(4), 742–759.

Lugones, M. (2012). Subjetividad esclava, colonialidad de género, marginalidad y opresiones múltiples. *Pensando los feminismos en Bolivia*, 129–140.

Marcos, S. (2009). Mesoamerican women's indigenous spirituality: Decolonizing religious beliefs. *Journal of Feminist Studies in Religion, 25*(2), 25–45.

Martí-Parreño, J., Méndez-Ibáñez, E., & Alonso-Arroyo, A. (2016). The use of gamification in education: A bibliometric and text mining analysis. *Journal of Computer-Assisted Learning, 32*(6), 663–676.

Martí, J. (2002). *José Martí: Selected writings.* New York, NY: Penguin.

Martín, D. (2017). Must reads: *Borderlands/La Frontera* by Gloria Anzaldúa. *Department of English at the University of California, Davis.* https://english.ucdavis.edu/news-events/news/must-reads-borderlandsla-frontera-gloria-anzaldúa

Mendez-Negrete, J. (2013). Pedagogical conocimientos: Self and other in interaction. *National Association for Chicana and Chicago Studies Annual Conference, 14*, 226–250.

Merriam-Webster. (n.d.). Act. In *Merriam-Webster.com Dictionary*. Retrieved November 16, 2021, from https://www.merriam-webster.com/dictionary/act

Merriam-Webster. (n.d.). Intercultural. In *Merriam-Webster.com Dictionary*. Retrieved November 16, 2021, from https://www.merriam-webster.com/dictionary/intercultural

Merriam-Webster. (n.d.). Words we're watching: 'Latinx' and gender inclusivity. In *Merriam-Webster.com Dictionary*. Retrieved November 16, 2021, from https://www.merriam-webster.com/words-at-play/word-history-latinx

Mignolo, W. (2005). *The idea of Latin America*. Malden, MA: Blackwell Publishing.

Moraga, C. (1997). The last generation. In A. M. García (Ed.), *Chicana feminist thought: The basic historical writings* (pp. 290–291). New York, NY: Routledge.

Moraga, C., & Anzaldúa, G. (2002). *This bridge called my back: Writings by radical women of color* (3rd ed.). Berkeley, CA: Third Woman Press.

Murillo Jr., E. G., Villenas, S., Galván, R. T., Muñoz, J. S., Martínez, C., & Machado-Casas, M. (Eds.). (2009). *Handbook of Latinos and education: Theory, research, and practice*. New York, NY: Routledge.

Navarro, M. (1989). The personal is political: Las Madres de Plaza de Mayo. In S. Eckstein (Ed.), *Power and popular protest: Latin American social movements* (pp. 241–258). Los Angeles, CA: University of California Press.

Navas, E., Gallagher, O., & Burrough, X. (2017). *Keywords in remix studies* (1st ed.). London, England: Taylor and Francis.

Omi, M., & Winant, H. (2015). *Racial formation in the United States* (1st ed.). New York, NY: Routledge.

Ortega, M. (2001). "New Mestizas," "World Travelers," and "Dasein": Phenomenology and the multi-voiced, multi-cultural self. *Hypatia, 16*(3), 1–29.

Ortega, M. (2016). *In-between: Latina feminist phenomenology, multiplicity, and the self.* Albany, NY: SUNY Press.

Ortiz, F., & Fernández, F. O. (1995). *Cuban counterpoint, tobacco and sugar*. Durham, NC: Duke University Press.

Pérez, E. (1999). *The decolonial imaginary: Writing Chicanas into history*. Bloomington, IN: Indiana University Press.

Pitts, A. J. (2016). Gloria E. Anzaldúa's autohistoria-teoría as an epistemology of self-knowledge/ignorance. *Hypatia, 31*(2), 352–369.

Pollock, D. (1998). Performing writing. In P. Phelan and J. Lane (Eds.), *The ends of performance* (pp. 73–103). New York, NY: Cultural Front.

Powell, H. C. (2017). Becoming a curator of memories: Memorializing memory as place in art making for art education. In A. Kantawala & P. Bolin (Eds.), *Revitalizing history: Recognizing the struggles, lives, and achievements of African American and women art educators* (pp. 27–40). Wilmington, DE: Vernon Press.

Reilly, B. (2012). Cold War transition: Europe's decolonization and Eisenhower's system of subordinate elites. In A. W. McCory, J. M. Fradera, and S. Jacobson (Eds.), *Endless empire: Spain's retreat, Europe's eclipse, America's decline* (pp. 344–359). Madison: University of Wisconsin Press, 2012.

Reilly, M., & Lippard, L. R. (2018). *Curatorial activism: Towards an ethics of curating*. Chicago, IL: Thames & Hudson.

Reyes, K. B., & Curry Rodríguez, J. E. (2012). Testimonio: Origins, terms, and resources. *Equity & Excellence in Education, 45*(3), 525–538.

Rosenblatt, L. M., & Booth, W. C. (1995). Literature as exploration (5th ed.). New York, NY: Modern Language Association of America.

Rouse, I. (1992). *The Taínos: Rise and decline of the people who greeted Columbus.* Hartford, CT: Yale University Press.

Saguê-Machiran, M. (2016). *Canoa: Taino indigenous dream river journey.* Bloomington, IN: iUniverse.

Saldívar-Hull, S. (1999). An interview with Gloria Anzaldúa. In G. Anzaldúa, *Borderlands: La frontera: The new mestiza* (2nd ed.) (pp. 233–34). San Francisco, CA: Aunt Lute Books.

Salinas Jr., C., & Lozano, A. (2017). Mapping and recontextualizing the evolution of the term Latinx: An environmental scanning in higher education. *Journal of Latinos and Education, 18*(4), 1–14.

Sandoval, C. (2013). *Methodology of the oppressed* (Vol. 18). Minneapolis, MN: University of Minnesota Press.

Schmidt, S. L. (2005). More than men in white sheets: Seven concepts critical to the teaching of racism as systemic inequality. *Equity & Excellence in Education, 38*(2), 110–122.

Smith, K. M. (2010). Female voice and feminist text: Testimonio as a form of resistance in Latin America. *Florida Atlantic Comparative Studies Journal, 12*(1), 21–37.

Sotomayor, L. (2016). Migration, race and identity: Arab migration and its impact on Cuban society through history and the visual arts. *Contextualizaciones Latinoamericanas,* 15. http://revistascientificas.udg.mx/index.php/CL/article/view/5931

Sotomayor, L. C. (2019). Uncrating josefina aguilar: Autohistoria and autohistoria-teoría in feminist curating of a muñecas series. *Studies in Art Education, 60*(2), 132–143.

Strayhorn, T. L. (2012). *College students' sense of belonging: A key to educational success for all students.* New York, NY: Routledge.

Sumra, M. K. (2019). Hormones and the human alpha female. *BioRxiv,* 697086.

Taylor, D. (1998). A savage performance: Guillermo Gómez-Peña and Coco Fusco's "Couple in the Cage." *TDR: The Drama Review, 42*(2), 160–175.

Trinidad Galván, R. (2016). Collective memory of violence of the female brown body: A decolonial feminist public pedagogy engagement with the feminicides. *Pedagogy, Culture & Society, 24*(3), 343–357.

Tuck, E., & Yang, K. W. (2012). Decolonization is not a metaphor. *Decolonization: Indigeneity, Education & Society, 1*(1), 1–40.

Vallone, M. (2014). The wound as bridge: The path of conocimiento in Gloria Anzaldúa's work. *E-rea: Revue électronique d'études sur le monde anglophone, 12*(1).

Velez, E. D. (2019). Decolonial feminism at the intersection: A critical reflection on the relationship between decolonial feminism and intersectionality. *Journal of Speculative Philosophy, 33*(3), 390–406.

Velez, E. D., & Tuana, N. (2020). Toward decolonial feminisms: Tracing the lineages of decolonial thinking through Latin American/Latinx feminist philosophy. *Hypatia, 35*(3), 366–372.

wa Thiong'o, N. (1998). Decolonising the mind. *Diogenes, 46*(184), 101–104.

Wilson, L. (2011). Artist's statement: Images of life: Witnessing atrocities. *Chicana/Latina Studies, 10*(2), 8–13.

Zaytoun, K. (2015). "Now let us shift" the subject: Tracing the path and post humanist implications of La Naguala/The Shapeshifter in the works of Gloria Anzaldúa. *MELUS, 40*(4), 69–88.

Further reading

Alarcón, N. (2006). Chicana feminism: In the tracks of "the" Native Woman. *Cultural Representation in Native America, 18,* 119.

Ashton, J. C. (Ed.) (2017). *Feminism and museums: Intervention, disruption and change* (Vol. 1). Cambridge, MA: MuseumEtc Ltd.

Bart, M. (2011). Critical reflection adds depth and breadth to student learning. *Faculty Focus.* https://www.facultyfocus.com/articles/teaching-and-learning/critical-reflection-adds-depth-and-breadth-to-student-learning/

Behar, R., & Gordon, D. A. (Eds.). (1995). *Women writing culture.* Berkeley, CA: University of California Press.

Berger, J. (2003). *Ways of seeing.* In A. Jones (Ed.), *The feminism and visual culture reader* (pp. 37–39). New York, NY: Routledge.

Bolin, P. E., & Kantawala, A. (Eds.). (2017). *Revitalizing history: Recognizing the struggles, lives, and achievements of African American and women art educators.* Wilmington, DE: Vernon Press.

Cantú, N. (2012). Getting there cuando no hay camino (when there is no path): Paths to discovery testimonios by Chicanas in STEM. *Equity & Excellence in Education, 45*(3), 472–487.

Cochran-Smith, M., & Lytle, S. L. (Eds.). (1993). *Inside/outside: Teacher research and knowledge.* New York, NY: Teachers College Press.

Colorado Mountain College. (2007). *Critical reflection.* http://faculty.coloradomtn.edu/orl/critical_reflection.htm

Eisner, E. W. (1993). Forms of understanding and the future of educational research. *Educational Researcher, 22*(7), 5–11.

Esteban-Guitart, M., & Moll, L. C. (2014). Funds of identity: A new concept based on the funds of knowledge approach. *Culture & Psychology, 20*(1), 31–48.

Femenía, N. A., & Gil, C. A. (1987). Argentina's mothers of Plaza de Mayo: The mourning process from junta to democracy. *Feminist Studies, 13*(1), 9–18.

Keating, A. (2013). *Transformation now: Toward a post-oppositional politics of change.* Urbana, IL: University of Illinois Press.

Lizárraga, H. R., & Gutiérrez, K. D. (2018). Centering nepantla literacies from the borderlands: Leveraging "in-betweenness." *Toward Learning in the Everyday: Theory into Practice, 57*(1), 38–47.

Lugones, M. (1987). Playfulness, "world"-travelling, and loving perception. *Hypatia, 2*(2), 3–19.

Marroquin, N., & Sotomayor, L. (2019). Talking about belonging and survival: An invitation. *Visual Arts Research, 45*(1), 46–55.

Omi, M., & Winant, H. (2009). Thinking through race and racism. *Contemporary Sociology, 38*(2), 121–125.

Parker, R., & Pollock, G. (1981). *Old mistresses: Women, art and ideology.* New York, NY: Pantheon Books.

Sieber, T. (2006). Knowledge, learning, and teaching: Striving for conocimiento. *Human Architecture: Journal of the Sociology of Self-Knowledge, 4*(3), 33.

Sotomayor, L. (2015). Harvest, roast, brew, and savor: Crafting auto-ethnographic research-based arts and arts-based research. *Visual Culture & Gender, 10,* 81–88.

Tarver, A. E. (2018). Eavesdropping. *Ecotone, 13*(2), 145–152.

Appendix A:
Glossary of terms

Anglo or White Americans: Anglos and/or White Americans are those who are not Hispanic or Latina/o origin, who speak the English language, including those who are not necessarily of English or British decent and live in the United States (Barber, 2010).

Chamana: Chamana is the feminine word in Spanish of shaman that Anzaldúa uses throughout her writings. (Anzaldúa, 2015, p. 223).

Chamanería: The Spanish word Chamaneria is used to describe shamanism as a system of healing through spiritual practice that is "more than forty thousand years old "(Anzaldúa, 2015, p. 223).

Colonization/colonizer: The action or process of establishing control over indigenous people is the act of colonizing; colonization by the colonizer, the peoples with power that are forcing control over another group of people.

Creative acts: I define the creative acts as deep, meaningful, embodied experiences that are woven into our mind, body, soul, and spirit manifesting through a creative vessel. For example, painting, music, writing, dance I consider as some forms of creative acts.

Critical reflection: Critical reflection is the act of deeply engaging inwardly to oneself about oneself. Critical reflection is a reasoning process that is descriptive, analytical, critical and through any articulated ways necessary. For example, creative acts, music, poetry, writing, art, etc. Critical reflection is integrated into the classroom and outside the classroom as a form of experiential learning where students respond through writing, art, and discussions before, during and after an experience analyzing multiple intersecting dimensions. I use a Critical Reflection process for interconnectedness addressing four specific areas: attention to multiple points of view, curate assignments/experiences for students with the awareness that critical reflection is a continuous process inside and outside the classroom beyond the allotted semester timeframe in college, engage students in critical reflection before, during, and after an experience, and facilitating meaningful discussions and seeds for further individual critical reflections (Jacoby, 2010).

Curando: Curando is the Spanish word for healing. I am using the word curando as a verb of an action occurring at some level, whether spiritually, physically, emotionally, or psychologically.

Curandera: Curandera is the Spanish word for a healer who uses folk medicines. In my Caribbean heritage, knowing or having a Curandera among family and social circles is common. A curandera may be any gender and is called upon to heal the body, mind, or spiritually through natural remedies found in the earth, through kinesthetic energies, intuition, and spiritual awareness.

Curator/Curadora: I situate curator in the Spanish word, curadora meaning someone who heals. In Latin, curator/curadora means guardian or trustee. I define curator/curadora in the context of this study as an umbrella term to include researcher, scholar, curator, facilitator, educator as the practice of curator as a researcher, contributing to the production of knowledge, theorizing, creating worlds, suggesting hypotheses, and proposing a form of narration or testimonios; generating a new perspective.

Curricular curation: I situate curricular curation to describe my approach through Anzaldúa's (2015) conocimiento theory and the seven transformative acts, as a guide for decolonizing educational spaces through emergent cultures of curriculum, which examines the various contexts of learning through sociopolitical, what is considered valuable content in art/design/epistemology, how/who is studied, and what is the organization of diverse educational (informal/formal) settings (Keifer-Boyd, 2019).

Desconocimiento: The Spanish word for lack of knowledge or things unknown is desconocimiento. Anzaldúa defines desconocimientos as "[s]mall acts of desconocimientos ignorance, frustrations, tendencies toward self-destructiveness, feelings of betrayal and powerless-ness, and poverty of spirit and imagination" (Anzaldúa, 2015, p. 154).

Entanglements: Wanda Knight (2007) writes about the historical and personal contexts that have been and are 'entangled' in the systemic oppression with the United States public educational system for both educators and students. The entanglements of race, class and gender that Knight writes about in her auto-ethnography helps to expose educational struggles, trauma, pain and the oppression felt by poor black females and the complexities of these entanglements.

Eurocentric framework: Eurocentric framework focuses on European culture and history exclusively as the center perspective for history, culture as surpassing all other cultures, history, and people.

Facilitator: I define a facilitator as an individual who guides conversations and curriculum in an educational environment.

Healing: Healing is the process of becoming whole in body, mind and spirit.

Healing through our wounds: I define healing through our wounds as the process of healing by going into our pain, hurts and wounds. Jung links the archetype of the Wounded Healer back to a Greek myth of antiquity. The myth of Chiron tells the story of how the centaur was wounded by an arrow from Heracles' bow. Chiron does not die; instead, he suffers excruciating pain for the rest of his life. Because of his wound, Chiron became known as a legendary healer in ancient Greece (Jung, 2014). Anzaldúa explains the process of healing when she writes, "In shadow work, the problem is part of the cure—you don't heal the wound; the wound heals you. First, you must recognize and acknowledge la herida. Second, you must "intend" to heal. Then you must fall headlong into that wounding—attend to what the body is feeling, be its dismemberment and disintegration. Rupture and psychic fragmentation lead to dialogue with the wound. In turn, dialogue opens imaginings, and images awaken an awareness of something greater than our individual wounds, enabling us to imagine ways of going through nepantla's disorientations to achieve wholeness and interconnect to others on the planet. And finally, you have to plunge your hands into the mess, plunge your hands en la masa, into embodied practical material spiritual political acts" (Anzaldúa, 2015, pp. 89–90).

Integration of diversity and inclusion: Lucy Lippard (1990), Andrea Herrera O'Reilly (2011), O'Reilly (2017), and Desai (2018), and many others have established that there is a difference between incorporating diversity as a recipe for color versus an embedded integration of diversity as part of the mosaic or fabric of a curriculum, art exhibit, etc.

Latino/a: I choose to use the term Latina/o throughout my research work because it is what I can pronounce in both Spanish and English as I go between two languages as a bilingual speaker. I find compelling the arguments made about imposing U.S./American social norms on other cultures by correcting the Spanish language and/or feeling the right to critique it, to begin with. Additionally, the term Latinx is non-existent in Spanish-speaking countries and is a U.S. invented term, serving U.S. context (Salinas & Lozano, 2017; M. de Onís, 2017).

Latinx: relating to, or marked by Latin American heritage —used as a gender-neutral alternative to Latino or Latina (Merriam-Webster, retrieved on February 23, 2020).

LGBTQA+: The LGBTQA+ (Lesbian, Gay, Bisexual, Trans, Queer, Ally and more) label is used at Penn State.

Náhuatl: Náhuatl is the indigenous language of the Aztec people.

Nepantlando: My collaboration and work with Dr. Christen Sperry García is developing a theoretical, conceptual framework using Gloria Anzaldúa's theory of conocimiento and nepantlera whereas educators and artists situate a third space of nepantlando as an activated place for the back and forth border crossings we engage in and with our students.

Non-Anglo perspectives: The readings that I introduced in the *Latina Feminisms* course center on non-Anglo perspectives and historically contextualize underrepresented people who are often excluded from or silenced by the dominant history (Knight, 2006).

Systemic Internalized Oppression (SIO): I define it as the systemic mistreatment of people within a social identity group that is supported and enforced by the society and institutions, laws, customs, and practices solely based on the person's membership to a social identity group. Systemic institutional oppression creates a homogenous, invisible system with barriers limiting people based on their membership to a marginalized social identity group and is only invisible to those unaffected by it. SIO is a result of these things regardless of intent. Institutions include legal, criminal justice systems, educational, health, government, media, and social services. Racial Formation theory was developed by Michael Omi and Howard Winant in the mid-1990s and is used to look at race as a social construction where the importance, content of racial categories are deterred by social, economic and political forces (Omi & Winant, 2015), Sheri Schmidt (2005) discusses seven foundational concepts to systemic inequality as: race as a social construction; dominant and subordinated groups; levels of racism; white privilege; internalized racism; multiple social group memberships; and historical inequality as applied to college classrooms for education. Through collaborative research and scholarship in psychology, the internalization of oppression within marginalized groups and how trauma can become part of the "psycho-spiritual internal fabric of human beings" (Duran, 2013, p. xiii). Eduardo Duran (2013) explains that in his experience as a psychologist working within a Western model, trauma is defined as occurring to physical and psychological layers of a person. It wasn't until his experiences led him to an indigenous group and he consulted with his root teacher from a native tradition that he came aware of the missing piece: spirit. He goes on to explain that the perpetrator passes on physical, emotional, and spiritual energy to the victims, which may also form into a lineage of trauma such as the genocide histories on Native and African populations in the United States.

Testimonio: Testimonio is the Spanish word for testimony; it has roots in oral cultures and Latin American human rights struggles. The genre of testimonios exposes brutality, disrupts silencing, and builds solidarity among women of color (Anzaldúa, 1990). Testimonios challenges objectivity by situating the individual in communion with a collective experience marked by marginalization, oppression, or resistance leading to new perspectives and knowledge building towards transformation, solidarity, and social justice (Delgado, Burciaga, & Carmona, 2012). Examples of testimonios; "I, Rigoberta Menchu: An Indian Woman" in *Guatemala/Me llamo Rigoberta Menchu, y as´i me nacio la consciencia* (Burgos-Debray, 2009). Si Me Permiten Hablar/Let Me Speak (Barrios de Chungara, 1978). Telling to Live (Latina Feminist Group, 2001) and as a means of expressing agency, for example, in This Bridge Called my Back (Moraga & Anzaldua, 1983) and ´ Gay Latino Histories/Dying to be Remembered (Roque Ramírez, 2010). In other cases, the narrative is used to locate social membership as racialized and classed subjects experiencing social mobility, such as Narratives of Mexican American Women (A. García, 2004), Voicing Chicana Feminisms (Hurtado, 2003), Migrant Daughter (Tywoniak & M. García, 2000) and Memories of Chicano History (M. García, 1994).

Transformative acts: I use the descriptor, transformative acts, as a phrase to describe the seven non-linear conocimiento stages.

Una herida abierta (an open wound): Gloria Anzaldúa uses the phrase, 'una herd abierta' to discuss the trauma and violence of the Texas/U.S. border and its impact psychologically, geographically, emotionally, culturally, and physically.

Wounds: Anzaldúa uses the metaphor of the wound in *Borderlands: La Frontera* (1999) as a way to explain and process her lived experiences within historical, political, cultural, social, linguistic, sexuality, race, ethnicity, ancestral, spiritual, religious, and gendered contexts (Vallone, 2014).

Appendix B:
Latina Feminisms course syllabus

Latina Feminisms 300: Latinas in the United States:
Gender, Culture, and Society

Course Syllabus

Instructor: Leslie C. Sotomayor (She, Her, Hers)

Fall 2018 | Tues./Thurs. 1:35–2:50 PM | Boucke 306

Office Hours: Tues. & Thursday 12:00–1:00 PM or by appointment

Office Location: Arts Cottage Graduate Offices

"I change myself; I change the world."– Gloria Anzaldúa

Course Description

This course will provide an overview of the intellectual contributions of Latina/Chicana feminists. In particular, we will look at the theoretical and political interventions of scholarship deeply rooted in women's lived experiences. We will participate in dialogue, inspire action, and put theory into practice in pioneering ways. We will examine the course's various themes through media, including nonfiction, fiction, poetry, film, art, theatre, music, popular culture, and personal/collective testimonios. This course pivots on Chicana activist Gloria Anzaldúa's groundbreaking theories of autohistoria-teoría and conocimiento. By studying and applying the seven transformative acts that comprise Anzaldúa's theory of conocimiento, each participant in the course will create their autohistoria.

Latinas form part of the fastest-growing ethnic group in this country, yet in most aspects of public, social, and cultural life, they remain largely underrepresented, often rendered invisible. This course will provide an in-depth understanding of Latina feminisms by exploring the various complex layers that make up the Latina experience in the United States. We will trace the dynamic historical transformations of Latinas in the United States and discuss Latinas' diverse identities and lives within specific cultural, historical, and social contexts.

We will discuss the multiplicity of Latina identities. How do entanglements of class, ethnicity, race, gender, and sexuality affect the daily experiences of Latinas? How do Latina feminists define their struggles and acts of political mobilization? What are the legacies of colonialism and imperialism that Latinas confront today? Through a careful analysis of the histories and experiences of Latinas, we will gain a greater understanding of the factors underlying Latinas' persistent marginalization and multiple oppressions. We will identify mechanisms of oppression and resistance to critique the large power structures and institutions in which Latinas are socially located. How do issues of language, work, family, migration, violence, and incorporation play out for these women in U.S. society?

*No phone usage is allowed during class time; no exceptions. Phones must be put away and out of sight.

***All readings are available through library reserves or Canvas.*

***You are required to bring readings/notes to class each week.

Required Text

Anzaldúa, G. (1999). *Borderlands: La frontera: The new mestiza* (2nd ed.). San Francisco, CA: Aunt Lute Books.

García, C. (1993). *Dreaming in Cuban: A novel.* New York, NY: Ballantine Books.

Recommended Text

Anzaldúa, G. (1990). *Making face, making soul: Haciendo caras: Creative and critical perspectives by feminists of color* (1st ed.). San Francisco, CA: Aunt Lute Books.

Moraga, C., & Anzaldúa, G. (Eds). (2015). *This bridge called my back: Writings by radical women of color* (4th ed.). Albany, NY: SUNY Press.

*This syllabus may change during the semester. Any changes will be discussed in class and reflected on Canvas.

**I allow one unexcused absence per semester. (An excused absence requires proof of absence, emailed to me before class or promptly after an emergency.) If you have a second unexcused absence, your final grade will be reduced by one letter. If you have a third absence, I will assume you have dropped the class.

Class Participation and Preparation with Blog Posts

Your attendance at and critical engagement during each class meeting is required. Active participation means regular attendance, careful and critical reading of class materials, involvement with in-class activities, and full engagement with lectures and discussions.

Participation (500 points)

– Participation requires that you are present and prepared for every class

Individual Class Blog

– Create an individual blog and send me the link

– Every Tuesday before class (unless otherwise noted on the syllabus), you will post on your blog a critical reflection on the week's readings using the "Critical Reading Tips" (below)

– Every Thursday during the final minutes of each class, you will post a critical reflection on the class discussions and assignments using the "Critical Reflection Tips" (below)

– Feel free to upload any links, images, art, doodles, or anything else that you would like to relate or connect to what you are reading and reflecting on to your blog

Class Facilitation

– You will plan and facilitate a class discussion that helps your classmates to engage with the readings.

– The goal of your lesson will be to identify the key points/arguments of the readings, foster discussion, build community, and increase engagement.

– You may be as creative as you like. For example, you might design an in-class activity or utilize media clips.

– **My day to facilitate class is_____.**

Critical Reading Tips

1. What is the thesis (i.e., statement of the problem) that the week's reading posits, and how does the author develop the ideas developed to make a case for the thesis?

2. Why is the thesis important, and for whom?

3. How does the author disclose their positionality in relation to the text?

4. What troubles you regarding the thesis and why?

5. How does or could the thesis of the reading connect to your life and work?

6. What ideas did you find particularly significant, powerful, or insightful, and why?

7. What questions arise from the reading that could help shape our class discussion?

Critical Reflection Tips

1. How did the class discussion make you feel?

2. Has anything changed in your thinking?

3. Did you feel at any point a sense of not belonging? Why or why not?

4. How did being an active listener make you feel? Did active listening change your perception?

5. Do you feel any healing or empathy because of this week's discussion, ideas, or assignments?

6. What is your reflection on this week's particular "act"?

Assignments (100 points each)

(Note: Each assignment will be shared and discussed in class.)

Biography/Profile of a Latina Presentation (sign up in class) ......Due 9/4

Identity Poem Presentation (any format or interpretation) ....Due 9/20

Testimonio ....…...... Due 10/9

Final Project: Curated Creative Poster (200 points)

– **Due on December 4, 2018, in class.**

– You are responsible for creating a creative poster representing any theme from class in correlation with Gloria Anzaldúa's book, *Borderlands*.

– Your creative digital poster should integrate theories, debates, and topics related to readings and discussions from class.

– You may incorporate ideas and themes from your lived experiences.

– Use only materials or readings on the syllabus.

– NO late posters will be accepted!

– Your poster should be an original design

– Your poster should have a mix of text and visual images

– Your poster should have a title

- Your poster may include video links, GIFs, or animation
- Your poster may be digital or a physical piece of artwork

Grading Scale

Grading is on a 1000-point scale (940–1000 A, 900–930 A-, 880–900 B+, 830–870 B, 800–820 B-, 770–790 C+, 700–760 C, 600–690 D, below 600 points F)

Dates & Topics Schedule

Recursive Transformative Stage 1: The Rupture/Susto

Week 1: 8/21 *Introduction, Context, Social Movements in the United States*

- Syllabus, name plates with pronouns, overview of history
- Sign up for Latina Profile
- Divide into groups for next class (A, B, C, D)
- Create your individual blog and send link to me; write your first post introducing yourself to the class

Week 1: 8/23 *What is Latina/o Studies?: Labels and Movements and Feminism*

- Gloria Anzaldúa and her theories of autohistoria-teoría and conocimiento
- Write your blog entry before class using "Critical Reading Tips"

Readings on Course Reserves:

hooks, b. (2014). *Feminism is for everybody: Passionate politics* (2nd. ed.). New York, NY: Routledge. Chapters 1–4.

Pérez, A. (2017). Practice and praxis: Chicana feminism and the history of the Chicana/Latina studies journal. *Diálogo, 20*(2), 55–66. Artist Spotlight: Maria Teresa Fernandez

Readings on Canvas:

Moraga, C., Anzaldúa, G., Tinker, J., & Bambara, T. C. (1983). *This bridge called my back: Writings by radical women of color.* Brooklyn, NY: Kitchen Table: Women of Color Press.

- Pick any three readings; include the titles of the three you chose in your blog and indicate why

Week 2: 8/30 *Historical Contexts and Activism*

Link:

http://www.chicanxdeaztlan.org/p/history.html (look specifically at the *History* and *About Us* sections)

Readings on Course Reserves:

González, B. J., & Loza, M. (2016). Opening the archives: Legacies of the bracero program. *Diálogo, 19*(2), 3–6. doi:10.1353/dlg.2016.0051

Fraser, H. M. (2008). "Los desaparecidos": The madres of the Plaza de Mayo and the reframing of the victims. *Canadian Woman Studies, 27*(1), 36.

http://palante.org/13%20Pt%20Program-Corrected.htm

Cofer, J. O. (2004). The myth of the Latin woman: I just met a girl named Maria. In Paula S. Rothenberg (Ed.), *Race, Class, and Gender in the United States: An Integrated Study* (pp. 203–207). New York, NY: Worth Publishers.

 – Critical Reflective Response blog post due

Week 3: 9/4 *Assignment #1 due, Latina Profile due*

 – In-class five-minute presentation

 – Critical Reading Response blog post due before class

Week 3: 9/6 Gloria Anzaldúa (1999), *Borderlands/La Frontera*

Readings: Foreword and Chapter 1

Facilitator:

 – Critical Reflective Response blog post due

Recursive Transformative Stage 2: Nepantla/The Tearing

Week 4: 9/11 *Border Theory and Entanglements*

Gloria Anzaldúa (1999), *Borderlands/La Frontera*

 – Reading: Chapter 2

 – Critical Reading Response blog post due

Week 4: 9/13 *Race*

Readings on Course Reserves:

Jansen, M. C. (2001). LatiNegras. *Frontiers, 22*(3), 168–183.

Cofer, J. O. The story of my body. In Latin Deli (pp. 135–146). London: University of Georgia Press.

Badillo, C. (2001). Only my hairdresser knows. *NACLA, 34*(6), 35–37.

Facilitator:

 – Critical Reflective Response blog post due

Recursive Transformative Stage 3: Despair

Week 5: 9/18 *Identity and Sexuality*

Gloria Anzaldúa (1999), *Borderlands/La Frontera*

Reading: Chapter 3

Week 5: 9/20 *Assignment #2 due (identity poem)*

Week 6: 9/25 *Sexuality*

Readings on Course Reserves:

Negron-Muntaner, F. (1999). When I was a Puerto Rican lesbian: Meditations on brincando el charco. *GLQ, 5*(4), 511–526.

- *Brincando el Charco* documentary
- Critical Reading Response blog post due before class

Week 6: 9/27 *Sexuality*

- Straight Talk Presentation: LGBTQ+
- Critical Reflective Response blog post due

Recursive Transformative Stage 4: Call to Action

Week 7: 10/2 *Invoking Art*

Gloria Anzaldúa (1999), *Borderlands/La Frontera*

Reading: Chapter 4

- Critical Reading Response due before class

Facilitator:

Week 7: 10/4 *Invoking Art*

Featured Artist: Diane Bienvades Rios

- Critical Reflective Response due

Recursive Transformative Stage 5: Autohistoria

Week 8: 10/9 *Our Testimonios*

Gloria Anzaldúa (1999), *Borderlands/La Frontera*

Reading: Chapter 5

- Critical Reading Response blog post due before class

Facilitator:

Week 8: 10/11 *Assignment #3 due (testimonio)*

- Share in class

- Critical Reflective Response blog post due

Recursive Transformative Stage 6: New Story to the World

Week 9: 10/16 *Rebuilding Ourselves*

Gloria Anzaldúa (1999), *Borderlands/La Frontera*

Reading: Chapter 6

- Critical Reading Response blog post due before class

Facilitator:

Week 9: 10/18 *Rebuilding Ourselves*

Ruth Bear

Readings at link: ruthbehar.com

- *Adio Kerida/Goodbye Dear Love* documentary

- Critical Reflective Response blog post due

Week 10: 10/23 *Violence, Borders, and Labor*

Readings on Course Reserves:

Moffatt, A. (2007). Murder, mystery and mistreatment in Mexican maquiladoras: It is never too late to make a difference. *Resources for Feminist Research, 32*(3–4), 223.

Wright, M. W. (2013). Feminicidio, narcoviolence, and gentrification in Ciudad Juárez: The feminist fight. *Environment and Planning D: Society and Space, 31*(5), 830–845. doi:10.1068/d17812

Grandia, L. (2015). Book review: *Enduring violence: Latina women's lives in Guatemala* by Cecilia Menjivar. *Journal of Latin American and Caribbean Anthropology, 20*(1), 182–184. doi:10.1111/jlca.12126

Facilitator:

Critical Reading Response blog post due before class

Week 10: 10/25 *Violence*

- Guest Speaker: Jennifer Pence

- Critical Reflective Response blog post due

Recursive Transformative Stage 7: Nepantlera/The Crosser/The Vision

Week 11: 10/30 *Becoming a Crosser*

Gloria Anzaldúa (1999), *Borderlands/La Frontera*

Reading: Chapter 7

- Critical Reading Response blog post due before class

Facilitator:

Week 11: 11/1 *Becoming a Crosser*

Gloria Anzaldúa (1999), *Borderlands/La Frontera*

Reading: Chapter 7

- Critical Reflective Response blog post due

Week 12: 11/6 *Visual Culture: Latinas in the Museum?*

Palmer Museum of Art Field Trip

- Meet at 1:35 PM in the second-floor print study room
- Critical Reading Response blog post due before class

Week 12: 11/8 *Popular Culture*

Readings on Course Reserves:

Gómez-Peña, G., & Mendieta, E. (2001). A Latino philosopher interviews a Chicano performance artist. *Nepantla: Views from South, 2*(3), 539–554.

Gómez-Peña, G. (1999). Mexican beasts, holy gang members, and wetbacks. *Theatreforum, 15*, 53.

Copeland, C. (2008). Art, gender, power, and the F word: An interview with Coco Fusco. *Afterimage, 35*(5), 4.

- *The Couple in The Cage* short film
- Critical Reflective Response blog post due

Week 13: 11/13 *Dreaming in Cuban*

- Reading: Section 1
- Critical Reading Response blog post due before class

Facilitator:

Week 13: 11/15 *Dreaming in Cuban*

- Reading: Section 2
- Critical Reading Response blog post due before class

Facilitator:

Week 14: 11/20 & 11/22: Fall Break: No Classes!

Week 14: 11/27 *Dreaming in Cuban*

- – Reading: Section 3
- – Critical Reading Response blog post due before class

Facilitator:

Week 15: 11/29 Finale of *Dreaming in Cuban*

- – Critical Reflective Response blog post due

Week 16: 12/4 Creative Poster Presentations

Week 16: 12/6 Creative Poster Presentations

Appendix C:
Latina Feminisms assignment description

Data Collection

I took field notes immediately following each class session. My field notes included sketches of the room layout, illustrations through sketches of conversations taking place, questions/comments/discussion posed by me or by students, notes, and my reflections and feelings. My field notes also included videos, poems, films, photos, or media shared in class by me or the students, including supplemental resources and materials used in addition to those listed on the syllabus. Students often engaged in class conversations before class officially began, as many arrived early or lingered after class in discussions. I also made a note of these in my reflections.

Blogs

Critical self-reflection is an integral part of transformative learning; therefore, critical writing, reflection, and reading are curated within the course. On the first day of class, students created a blog on any platform of their choice. On their private from public-view blogs, they documented their personal journey throughout the semester. Students sent their URL link to me, as I am the only one that read their blog entries. Students were to include an initial entry introducing themselves, why they are taking the class, and preferred pronouns. Students documented their experiences by journaling about the class readings and discussions via their personal blog sites. Each week students created and uploaded two blog journal entries using (if they choose) the guidelines delineated in the critical reading tips developed by art educator Karen Keifer-Boyd[1] and critical reflection discussion tips (see section on the syllabus in Appendix A). Each Tuesday, students posted a critical reflection about the course readings using the course critical reading tips (see a section of the syllabus in Appendix A) to guide their responses. Every Thursday, the students posted a critical response drawing on their reflections on that week's discussions, also guided by critical reflection tips.

---

[1] Keifer-Boyd posts these critical reading tips for students in her courses, for example, at http://cyberhouse.arted.psu.edu/difference/projects/1_overlap.html

Assignments

I intentionally left the assignments open to interpretation as not to hinder students' creativity and possibilities towards new perspectives. Students had initial apprehensions to the freedoms with each assignment since, according to them, "that never happens in other classes." To ease learners' apprehensions, we discussed each assignment in advance as a group to alleviate any anxiety and brainstorm concepts. For example, for the testimonio assignment, we discussed the diverse readings of testimonios we had done in class up to that point and how one's individual testimony should be a manifestation of their lived experiences. For the final creative poster project, we dedicated part of a class session (this was improvised and not part of the syllabus originally) to going around the class circle and sharing preliminary ideas for each student's creative poster. Additionally, we commented on any thoughts or questions as each person shared their conceptual ideas. Taking the time to brainstorm in the group setting allowed students to further reflect on synthesizing a thesis for their theme(s), connections to Anzaldúa and other course readings, and the visual interpretations for designing their posters.

Facilitation

Each student signed up for a day to facilitate a class discussion. The student incorporated any materials they felt necessary or desirable that correlated with the topic and readings for that given week. The goal of the facilitating is to identify the key points/arguments of the readings, foster discussion, build community, and increase engagement. Facilitating a class discussion allows for student participation, active listening, their voice to emerge in a leadership role, and belonging to the class discussion through a new perspective. I noticed that students often were very creative with how they went about facilitating a class discussion and interjected their own lived experiences. For example, one student brought in additional readings and shed light on the research work of Gershen Kaufman and his book, *Shame: The Power of Caring* (1980), which Anzaldúa credits for her understanding of the subject and refers to in *Borderlands* (1999). Another student connected the *Borderlands* (1999) chapter, "Entering the Serpent," to her disciplinary field of reproductive rights. In guiding students to make broader connections of course themes without many restrictions but with creative freedom, students developed their own lens to 'read' Anzaldúa's work in relation to their own lived and living experiences.

Latina/o Research Presentation

The first assignment that students are responsible for is a Latina/o/x research presentation. During the first week of class, each student chose a name from a list of Latinx individuals I circulated in class. Each student was responsible for researching their chosen person, creating a 5-minute presentation about them, and sharing it with the class. This assignment is important at the beginning of the semester for students to get to know each other, as they have a short Q & A time after each presentation inspiring dialogue. Furthermore, this assignment also serves as a foundation for the gaps in our knowledge, to see the diverse Latinx individuals that may not be part of the traditional academic canon, and to make connections with students' lived experiences. For example, students related many of their presentations to their own culture, homelands, heritage, and passions in their life.

Identity Poems

Students wrote identity poems about any part of themselves that they felt comfortable sharing. Each student had creative liberty to present their identity poem in any format they'd like with no time restraint. This is the second assignment of the semester, and the purpose of me curating into the syllabus as such is to facilitate students learning more about each other, themselves, and dialogue with one another towards intimacy and relationship-building. I realized that students shared parts of themselves that were vulnerable and also painful aspects of their identities, such as; traumatic past experiences, violence, and feelings of not belonging. Students were free to discuss afterward, reserving the right not to answer or discuss any part of themselves that they did not feel comfortable with. I noticed an empathic sense around the circle in listening to fragments of each other's lives. Students commented on how "from the outside we wouldn't know these things about each other, we go through the whole semester sitting next to people not really knowing them, but this is different, I see you all differently now" (P.R. 2018). In students hearing each other, a reverence was felt in our classroom as active listeners.

Testimonios

One of the main topics we discussed in the *Latina Feminisms* class is that of our lived experiences, re-writing our narratives (autohistoria) and our testimonios. Students engaged in reading, viewing, and listening to testimonios of various interpretations through performative art, short films in class (Aja Monet, for example) and reading excerpts from *This Bridge Called My Back* (2002) poetry by Lorna Dee Cervantes and Julia Alvarez. Testimonios are an expression of something an individual has experienced or witnessed that has somehow impacted or transformed their life. Students wrote their own testimonios and shared them in class. Sharing part of one's testimonio is a sharing of vulnerable experiences, often emotional and a steppingstone in healing through our wounds.

Creative Poster

The final project for the course was for each student to create their own creative poster engaging with a theme(s) from Anzaldúa's *Borderlands* (1999) during the semester and/or lived experiences. Students were encouraged to take inventory of past assignments, class discussions, and blog entries to reflect on their journey thus far and begin to articulate a new vision for themselves and the world.

Index

CPSIA information can be obtained
at www.ICGtesting.com
Printed in the USA
LVHW082327160222
711352LV00009B/58/J